Using Technology Improve Adolescent Writing

Digital Make-Overs for Writing Lessons

Liz Campbell Stephens

Texas State University-San Marcos

Kerry H. Ballast

Central Texas Writing Project

PEARSON

Boston Columbus Indianapolis New York San Francisco Upper Saddle River
Amsterdam Cape Town Dubai London Madrid Milan Munich Paris Montreal Toronto
Delhi Mexico City Sao Paulo Sydney Hong Kong Seoul Singapore Taipei Tokyo

To Richard Sterling,
whose speech at the 2005 Annual Meeting of
the National Writing Project
inspired us, and whose leadership opened doors
for present and future educators to explore writing in digital ways

---

Vice President, Editor-in-Chief: Aurora Martínez Ramos
Editorial Assistant: Amy Foley
Director of Marketing: Chris Flynn
Marketing Manager: Amanda Stedke
Production Editor: Gregory Erb
Editorial Production Service: DB Publishing Services, Inc.
Manufacturing Buyer: Megan Cochran
Electronic Composition: Schneck-DePippo Graphics
Interior Design: Debbie Schneck
Cover Designer: Linda Knowles

For Professional Development resources visit www.pearsonpd.com.

10 9 8 7 6 5 4 3 2 1 RRD-VA 14 13 12 11 10

www.pearsonhighered.com

ISBN-10: 0-13-158735-8
ISBN-13: 978-0-13-158735-9

Contents

Chapter 3 Responsive Writing   51

Chapter 4 Purposeful Writing   79

Chapter 5 Social Action Writing   107

Chapter 6 Ten of Tens   135

Foreword

New Opportunities for Writing and Its Teaching: Thinking Digitally

What would it take to turn exceptional writing instruction into everyday classroom practice?

Richard Sterling, Chair, National Advisory Panel:
The National Commission on Writing. *Writing and School Reform*

For the past several years I have served with Liz Stephens on the National Advisory Panel for the National Commission on Writing as we've confronted the challenges that inevitably attend writing and its teaching. At our meetings, I have enjoyed listening to Liz talk about her remarkable work with the National Writing Project (NWP), all the while anticipating the ways in which the NWP and its teachers were sure to inform her and Kerry Ballast's emerging book. I was not disappointed. Each chapter of *Using Technology to Improve Adolescent Writing* grounds itself in theoretical contentions that expand teacherly views of learning while at the same time pointing to innovative and effective classroom practices. A daunting accomplishment to be sure. The pages of Stephens and Ballast's comprehensive book demonstrate that digital media—when incorporated thoughtfully into everyday school activities—can abet the teaching and learning of writing in an extraordinary fashion. Their book goes far in addressing how, as Richard Sterling asks in the epigraph, all writing instruction can be exemplary and how, moreover, digital media can contribute to this excellence.

As I write, my colleagues and I are in the middle of hosting the University of Illinois NWP Summer Institute, and I have the pleasure every day of meeting and writing with twenty teaching fellows and teacher consultants. As I sit here this morning among all the other writers with their laptops, I am struck by how thoroughly *Using Technology to Improve Adolescent Writing* takes up core NWP practices and transforms them to meet the challenge of 21st century literacies. Core activities that mark the NWP summer institutes include not only time devoted to participants' own writing, as Jim Gray (2000) pointed out long ago. If we are to teach writing we must be writers ourselves. We must also take up professional reading and then bring the writing and reading together in a teaching demonstration. The demonstration becomes far more than a sample class outline as teaching fellows fold into their practice much that they themselves have learned from their own research during the four weeks of institute participation. At the University of Illinois Writing Project site, as at the Central Texas site that Stephens and Ballast have led, we also infuse these activities at every opportunity with digital media, asking participants to develop critical questions as to how they may productively apply—or not—digital approaches to their teaching and writing. Through the use of digital media, we explore, as Stephens and Ballast explain, "what the writing process means when writing includes words, images, sound, video, animation" and more.

Every page of *Using Technology to Improve Adolescent Writing* opens up new worlds for writing and the teaching of writing. The book distinguishes itself in many ways, but certainly its pedagogically sound consideration of Web 2.0 tools warrants attention. Anyone who has written and responded to blogs, participated in a wiki, friended family and colleagues on Facebook, followed or been followed by those on Twitter (or its teen equivalent, Plurk) is likely to recognize the qualitative change in producing multiple textual objects for a variety of audiences and often with less expertise than one might expect. Writing emails to another individual or group will always, I believe, be special to those of us who came online in the early 1980s. But today some of the new Web 2.0 tools enable us to post a variety of text objects with an ease hitherto unknown. Sound, images, video, and alphabetic text all come together and are read by strangers and intimates alike, sometimes halfway across the globe. The sheer enormity of the number of people who contribute regularly to these sites suggests that teachers and students need to bring these social media into the classroom as both tools and objects of study. Statistics from January 2009 on the attention these sites receive from people around the world are impressive and have continued to grow. Adam Singer (2009) presents us with a snapshot:

> 1,000,000,000,000 (one trillion)—approximate number of unique URLs in Google's Search index
>
> 684,000,000—number of visitors to Wikipedia in 2008
>
> 112,486,327—number of views of the most viewed video on YouTube (January 2009)
>
> 346,000,000—number of people globally who read blogs (comScore, March 2008)
>
> 2,482,745,762—number of tweets on Twitter as of July 6, 2009, 9:45 CDT
>
> 150,000,000—number of active Facebook users

And it's not just the numbers that startle and surprise. More than anything the possibilities that Web 2.0 tools offer alongside the rising number of participants begin to change the way we think about writing and learning. When we add to the statistics the following statement from John Seely Brown and Richard Adler's "Minds on Fire," the potential for students' learning through Web technologies begins to become apparent:

> The original World Wide Web—the "Web 1.0" that emerged in the mid-1990s—vastly expanded access to information. . . . But the Web 2.0, which has emerged in just the past few years, is sparking an even more far-reaching revolution. Tools such as blogs, wikis, social networks, tagging systems, mashups, and content-sharing sites are examples of a new user-centric information infrastructure that emphasizes participation (e.g., creating, re-mixing) over presentation, that encourages focused conversation and short briefs (often written in a less technical, public vernacular) rather than traditional publication, and that facilitates innovative explorations, experimentations, and purposeful tinkerings that often form the basis of a situated understanding emerging from action, not passivity. (2008, p. 30)

This kind of participation—with its tremendous potential for learning and writing—is something that as educators and writing teachers we want to be able to tap into, but we don't always know how. Stephens and Ballast's book goes far in showing us the "how" of teaching writing in Web 2.0 environments.

In introducing their book, Stephens and Ballast ask us, "Since teens are reading, writing, and creating extensively on the Web, shouldn't educators explore how they are doing that?" For sure. The Web has indeed become the setting for many teens' (and adults') literacy practices and should not be neglected as an invaluable resource. Whereas at one time most of us were primarily "viewers"—we browsed the Web at will—today many, including, or perhaps especially, teens, are "doers" in this new literacy environment (Hawisher, 2000). As the authors point out, the Web has become a read-write environment where individuals can easily—without specialized and expensive software—create and distribute words and images to be read and responded to by friends, classmates, and teachers, who, in turn, can craft responses sometimes with alphabetic text but often with sound or even video that they simply select and upload, say, to their student's or classmate's blog or other site. Some students and teachers will make videos of their responses without ever moving from their laptop or desktop computer while others might use relatively inexpensive Flip cameras or mobile phones. Regardless of the specific choice of technology, Stephens and Ballast would have teachers and their students take advantage of these relatively new Web 2.0 educational opportunities.

In their preface, Stephens and Ballast explain some of the impulses that may have prompted them in *Using Technology to Improve Adolescent Writing* to take already excellent teaching plans and redo them through the appropriate use of digital media. They essentially seek to make good lessons better through an infusion of technology but also by positioning them within well-honed theoretical perspectives. More than merely adding a shot of technology to the mix, this collection of "make-overs" demonstrates more clearly than other teaching books I've encountered just how theory can be transformed and applied in the day-to-day workings of a class. The authors include, for example, an impressive array of analytical frameworks, which they name simply "frames." These frames consist of *inside writing*, *responsive writing*, *purposeful writing*, and *social action writing*—all of which are embedded in the ways in which the profession thinks about "writing processes" but also which expand thinking in interesting ways. *Inside writing* can be thought of as primarily "prewriting" or "invention" but has the added requirement of encouraging total student engagement always in their writing and research; *responsive writing* has to do with collaboration but also asks students to engage earnestly with one another, online and off, on a variety of problem-solving tasks and sometimes with students across the globe; *purposeful writing* relates to writing, arrangement, and even style but also cuts across different kinds of texts that may be alphabetic but also include still and moving images among other media objects; and, finally, *social action writing* touches the whole and can be related to Aristotle's deliberative rhetoric in which students bring attention to a pressing issue and encourage others to act, again through a variety of texts that cut across media. Theorists included and explained clearly in the book are educational thinkers Jerome Bruner, John Dewey, Paulo Freire, Seymour Papert, Jean Piaget, as well as those who have over the years immersed themselves in our own field of Writing Studies: Arthur Applebee, Deborah Appleman, Lucy Calkins, Harvey Daniels, Janet Emig, Donald Graves, Thomas Kent, Judith Langer, Ken Macrorie, Donald Murray, and more.

On top of presenting exciting, theoretically grounded ideas for teaching writing, the authors include lots of additional great resources. Did you know, for example, that there's a Son of Citation Machine (www .citationmachine.net) to help students (and teachers) with their bibliographies? A free online survey tool (www.surveymonkey.com)? TeacherTube (www.teachertube.com), a site that provides video resources and sample lessons? Or even a free blog especially available to educators that students and teachers can easily use (http://edublogs.org/)? Do you know about Google Apps (a combination of various collaborative tools) www.google .com/apps, FreeMind (Concept Mapping) http://freemind.sourceforge.net/ wiki/index.php/Main-Page, and VoiceThread (image, document, and video sharing) http://voicethread.com? And these are just a few of the many excellent websites and teaching ideas presented in *Using Technology to Improve Adolescent Writing*.

Next year, as my colleagues and I work together on the University of Illinois Writing Project Summer Institute, I plan to include Stephens and Ballast's remarkable book. Overall their work here does more than merely introduce us to new digital media: it helps us imagine how Web 2.0 tools might be used profitably in connection with our classes. There is simply no other text out there like it.

Gail E. Hawisher
University of Illinois, Urbana-Champaign
October, 2009

References

Brown, J. S., & Adler, R. P. (2008). Minds on fire: Open education, the long tail, and learning 2.0. *Educause. January/February*. www.johnseelybrown.com/. Retrieved 5 July 2009.

Gray, J. (2000). *Teachers at the center: A memoir of the early years of the national writing project*. Berkeley, CA: National Writing Project.

Hawisher, G. E. (2000). Accessing the virtual worlds of cyberspace. *Journal of Electronic Publishing*. http://quod.lib.umich.edu/cgi/t/text/text-idx?c=jep;view=text;rgn=main;idno=3336451.0006.106. Retrieved July 12, 2009.

Singer, A. (2009). Social media, web 2.0 and internet stats. http://thefuturebuzz. com/2009/01/12/social-media-web-20-internet-numbers-stats/. Retrieved July 5, 2009.

Writing and School Reform. (2006). Report of the National Commission on Writing. New York: College Board.

Preface

What began as a light comment about what would be the best way to help middle and high school teachers reenvision the teaching of writing resulted in a book that has truly been a journey. We thought, wouldn't it be great to do make-overs for lessons like the make-overs that are done for people and homes on popular TV shows? The idea of a make-over captured the seriousness of what we are seeing as a transitional time in writing instruction. With the advent of Web 2.0 tools, cell phones, and a social networking phenomenon, writing has become a part of the adolescent growth experience in ways that it never has been in the past. Certainly, generations before now exchanged notes in class and wrote letters to each other, but most of the daily exchange of ideas was relegated to telephone conversations with friends and family who typically lived in the same town or city. Communicating in the 21st century inevitably leads to writing—writing text messages, writing instant messages, writing email messages, writing in Web spaces like wikis and blogs. Writing is how teens communicate, not only with friends in their area but with teens across the world. We feel strongly that bringing an awareness of this mode and expanse of communication to all classrooms is critical and that the transition from thinking about writing on paper with a pen to writing in digital ways must take center stage in teacher preparation and professional development. We hope that our exploration of how that transition might begin—by a make-over of an existing method of teaching writing—might help to engage our students (and our teachers) in learning in the 21st century.

Acknowledgments

We are grateful to so many who have led and supported us through this journey. Many do not know how influential they were to us—from the leaders in our field to teachers we have known to the students we have taught. Gail Hawisher and Cynthia Selfe, who have for more than two decades investigated what writing with computers means, blazed trails for research and publications. Their work and the work of scholars inspired by them have guided us for several years. The teacher consultants of the National Writing Project, who have moved on the edge of innovation, have inspired us to ask questions that sometimes can only be answered with more questions. We interact in a constant state of inquiry. Our students—both at the 6–12 level and college level—have allowed us to experiment, to try new ways to approach their learning. The pages in this book can only hint at the volumes that we have gained from these friends.

We are grateful, too, to the editors and their assistants who guided us along the way. Linda Bishop launched our work with a phone call that invited us to pursue our proposal for this book. Her guidance was invaluable. Aurora Martínez Ramos helped us to finalize our manuscript and address the needs of our readers with clarity. We are most grateful to the reviewers who read our drafts and offered insightful and rich comments: Heather E. Bruce, University of Montana; Jacqueline N. Glasgow, University of Ohio; and Cynthia Rogers, Fairmont Junior High. Most important, we are grateful to our families for their patience, support, and coaching.

chapter 1

Writing in a Digital Age

It's hard to mess up on a computer.

Hector, grade 11

Our secondary students are growing up in interesting times. Consider the following news items:

- Business moves to social networking systems—Facebook, a social networking system that began in a Harvard dorm room in 2004 for college students to stay in touch, is a $15 billion enterprise where businesses like Apple, Inc., Intel Corp., Microsoft Corp., PepsiCo., Inc., and Starbucks Corp. have set up shop.

- Micro-blogging services are experiencing colossal growth and surpassing social networking systems like Facebook. Micro-blogging allows people to send very short messages to "followers" online. Twitter grew by 1,384 percent between 2008 and 2009, and although teens were not the largest user group among the 7 million unique visitors, teens have their own version of Twitter called Plurk.

- McDonald's adds digital toys to Happy Meals—McDonald's has traded the plastic figure in its Happy Meals for a digital CD-ROM game called Fairies and Dragons—a game that is targeted to children between seven and nine years old but accessible to children younger and older than that. Polls show that only 3 percent of elementary students do *not* play electronic games on some kind of device, compared to 9 percent of middle school students and 17 percent of high schoolers (Project Tomorrow, 2008).

- Teens drop out because they are bored—Almost one-third of all teens do not graduate from high school. Nearly half of those interviewed for *The Silent Epidemic* (n.d.), a national survey of self-identified dropouts, said a major reason for dropping out was that they were bored and disengaged from school. More than 80 percent said their chances of staying in school would have increased if classes were more interesting and provided opportunities for real-world learning.

- Teens are e-business owners—A study by the Global Entrepreneurship Monitor showed that the United States was unusual among developed countries in having a higher business start-up rate among its 18- to 24-year-olds than its 35- to 44-year-olds (Schoof, 2006). Six in every ten teens want to be an entrepreneur, and they can start e-businesses with little or no capital, according to www.entrepeneur.com, thanks to philanthropic support. Several teens have accrued tens of thousands of dollars with their e-businesses.

- Writing can determine job opportunities—Writing precisely, whether on paper or digitally, is a life skill and something that adults in just about all professions and careers do. It opens pathways for success, and it is how opportunities are gained or lost. The National Commission on Writing's report (2004) on writing in the workplace states that "in today's workplace writing is a 'threshold skill' for hiring and promotion among salaried (i.e., professional) employees" (p. 3).

Although this 21st century version of the old newsreels may appear to be a random collection, the items are integrally connected. Each news item can generate rich dialogue regarding the implications for teaching and learning in the secondary schools. For instance, if the corporate community is moving toward social networking systems and teens are the experts on social networking systems, shouldn't we regard sites like Facebook differently in schools? Is McDonald's move to video game prizes in the Happy Meal a sign of how much the next group of teens will know and do technologically? Are teens bored because what they do in school does not relate to their interests and habits outside of school? Since teens are reading, writing, and creating extensively on the Web, shouldn't educators explore how they are doing that? And shouldn't teachers attempt to bring that venue into the classroom? Where does writing fit in all of this? Clearly, it fits in all of it, but just how essential and consequential a skill is writing in the digital age? So, individually, the news items point to pressing questions regarding instruction in today's classroom, and together, these items forecast a learning environment that will look, sound, and feel very different from most of our classrooms.

Purpose for This Book

When we initially imagined a book on how to teach writing in the secondary classroom, we looked at what the professional as well as popular literature had to say about literacy in the digital age. We also considered our combined experience teaching and mentoring teachers, novice teachers in particular. Both of us taught English/language arts in middle and high school, studied technology and literacy, provided professional development for teachers, and continue to be active in the National Writing Project. From our experience and training in literacy, technology, and teacher education emerged a number of questions about how writing is changing in the digital age. Our query mainly focused on what the writing *process* means when writing includes words as well as images, sound, video, animation, and other electronic elements. In an effort to make sense of what we know, we developed what we are calling *frames of the writing process*: inside writing, responsive writing, purposeful writing, and social action writing. These will be discussed more fully later in this chapter.

After a wide review of resources for teaching writing, we determined a number of ways to couch the delivery of our message, and we outlined possible conceptualizations of the purpose for this book:

1. To shed light on the issues surrounding the implementation of technology in the classroom, in particular, those issues that emerge from identified obstacles such as lack of equipment, lack of professional development, the digital divide, etc.

2. To provide a "recipe book" of lessons to show teachers how to implement technology in writing instruction, step by step.

3. To recognize how secondary school students are proficient with technology and to think of ways to motivate them using digital tools that they use outside of school.

We decided to take the third approach—to imagine students as tech-savvy and to rethink how we see the ubiquitous *writing process* instruction that has permeated our K through college pedagogy for more than twenty-five years. Much has happened regarding how we write and what we use to write with in that time, and signs of a continuing transformation are emerging. College courses, for example, have titles that look very different from those of the 1970s and 1980s, like "Digital Media and English Studies" (Ohio State University), "Multimedia Writing" (University of Iowa), and "Digital Literature" (Yale University). Some traditionally titled courses like "Rhetoric and Composition" have course descriptions that include words like *wiki*, *blog*, and *multimodal*—terms that just a few years ago were not part of our lexicon. Clearly the effect of the digital age on the act of communicating is being recognized at the tertiary levels of education, where courses reflect an evolving perspective on what it means to be literate. It's time to consider new perspectives at the secondary level, where the digital natives are.

Who Are Digital Natives?

In his book *Don't Bother Me, Mom, I'm Learning* (2006), Marc Prensky writes: "How should we refer to this new generation of young people? Some call them the N-[for Net]-gen, the D-[for digital]-gen, or the Millenials. But the most useful term I have found for them is *Digital Natives*—the new 'native speakers' of the digital language of computers, video games, and the Internet" (p. 28).

Prensky describes the "digital immigrants" as those who are not teens and who may understand technology but still speak with an accent. Given this view of natives and immigrants, Prensky argues that educators must recognize and value how teens learn, particularly while they are playing complex video games. Adding the elements of gameplay to education, he explains, will keep middle school digital natives motivated because gameplay presents continual physical, intellectual, and emotional challenges, something digital natives crave.

Prensky's characterization of the digital native is substantiated by the work of the Pew Research Center, a nonprofit "fact tank" that provides information on the impact of the Internet on children, families, communities, the workplace, schools, health care, and civic/political life. Approximately 1,000 teens age 12 to 17 and their parents or guardians were interviewed in 2007 (Lenhart, Madden, Macgill, & Smith, 2007). Nearly all of the teens (94 percent) said they use the Internet, and more of them than ever are using it to share creations, tell stories, and interact with others. The number of digital natives who are creating these digital products is growing each year. About two-thirds of them have created and uploaded at least one of the following onto a Web page or blog (online journals): artwork, videos, stories, photos. The findings show that the number of teens who have created blogs has increased significantly—from 19 percent in 2004 to 28 percent in 2007 (Lenhart et al., 2007). Nearly the same number has remixed content captured online to design their creations. More than half of these digital natives have created a profile on a social networking site such as Facebook or MySpace, and 14 percent of them have posted videos. It is interesting to note that the 2007 survey was the first time the Pew researchers included questions about video posting and sharing. World Wide Web creator Sir Tim Berners-Lee, if he has reviewed this and other reports, is likely smiling in affirmation of his dream, a read-write Internet, one commonly known as Web 2.0:

> For years I had been trying to address the fact that the web for most people wasn't a creative space; there were other editors, but editing web pages became difficult and complicated for people. What happened with blogs and with wikis, these editable web spaces, was that they became much more simple. When you write a blog, you don't write complicated hypertext, you just write text, so I'm very, very happy to see that now it's gone in the direction of becoming more of a creative medium. (Lawson, 2005)

We know that teens are using the read-write Web. They are also IMing, texting, and tweeting (using Twitter). When they communicate on the Web or through a mobile device like a cell phone, they are using words to express themselves—they are writing. However, in many cases, they are also using graphics, photos, video, and sound when they write with words. Their creative process, then, is multimodal. Given that they are using a digital platform for writing in multimodal ways, unlike any other generation of teens before them, how do these digital natives view the act of writing with words? The Pew Research Center and the National Commission on Writing set out to answer this question. Not surprisingly, digital natives distinguish in-school writing from out-of-school writing. What may be surprising is that they do not consider the six to eight hours a week that they spend, on the average, composing messages online and creating multimodal products to be *real* writing. According to the executive summary of the survey, "The act of exchanging emails, instant messages, texts, and social network posts is communication that carries the same weight to teens as phone calls and between-class hallway greetings" (Lenhart et al., 2007). For the most part, they greatly enjoy nonschool writing—more than half of them said they enjoy it "a great deal," in fact. In striking contrast, only 17 percent said they enjoy writing at school. Despite that, a majority of teens do recognize the importance of good writing skills for success in life. They also say they are most motivated to write in school when they can select topics that are relevant to their lives and interests and when they are challenged and supported by engaged adults. One finding in this report's data, the piece that the news media found most intriguing, is that digital natives recognize and accept the informality of their online writing (using text shortcuts like LOL in texting and emoticons, for instance) and admit that they occasionally incorporate that informal style into their in-school writing (see Table 1.1).

To situate the digital native in a larger perspective, consider the results of an expansive national study by Project Tomorrow, a nonprofit organization dedicated to the preparation of youth for 21st century jobs/careers (Project Tomorrow, 2008). Since it began in 2003, Project Tomorrow has polled more than 1.2 million K–12 students, teachers, administrators, and parents representing over 14,000 schools in all fifty states through its annual Speak Up Project. The most recent data, collected in 2007, was drawn from communities surrounding the 3,729 schools that participated in the survey. Nearly all of the schools polled are public (3 percent private), more than 40 percent are Title I eligible, and nearly a third have majority-minority populations. The distribution of schools in urban, suburban, and rural settings

Table 1.1 *Writing, Technology, and Teens:* Summary of Findings at a Glance

Even though teens are heavily embedded in a tech-rich world, they do not believe that communication over the Internet or text messaging is writing.
The impact of technology on writing is hardly a frivolous issue because most believe that good writing is important to teens' future success.
Teens are motivated to write by relevant topics, high expectations, an interested audience, and opportunities to write creatively.
Writing for school is a nearly everyday activity for teens, but most assignments are short.
Teens believe that the writing instruction they receive in school could be improved.
Nonschool writing, while less common than school writing, is still widespread among teens.
Multichannel teens and gadget owners do not write any more—or less—than their counterparts, but bloggers are more prolific.
Teens more often write by hand for both out-of-school writing and school work.
As tech-savvy as they are, teens do not believe that writing with computers makes a big difference in the quality of their writing.
Parents are generally more positive than their teen children about the effect of computers and text-based communication tools on their child's writing.
Teens enjoy nonschool writing and, to a lesser extent, the writing they do for school.

Source: Lenhart, A., Arafeh, S., Smith, A., & Macgill, A. R. *Writing, Technology and Teens,* Washington, DC: Pew Internet & American Life Project, April 24, 2008. Reprinted with permission.

was nearly even. A composite of the American teen population described in this data suggests the following:

- Most secondary school students consider themselves "average" in their technology skills as compared to their peers.

- Gaming is the most popular use of technology among all students, followed by downloading music and social networking.

- Most high school students have a personal website like MySpace or Facebook; nearly half of middle school students do.

- In school, secondary students use technology most often for writing and doing online research.

Although teachers and administrators highly support the idea that technology enhances student achievement, administrators feel more positive than teachers do about their schools' adequately preparing students for jobs of the digital age. And students are even less positive. More than three-quarters of the students who identified themselves as advanced users of technology felt that their schools are not preparing them for future jobs. Project Tomorrow researchers suggest the existence of a chasm separating teen and adult perspectives regarding the role of technology in schools. Mobile computing devices such as cell phones, MP3 players, iPods, and PDAs are more popular each year, and secondary school students are increasingly frustrated with campus rules that limit access and restrict, if not prohibit, use of the very tools and devices that they "use constantly outside of school . . . in all aspects of their lives" (p. 7). That discontent factor has grown by 46 percent between 2003 and 2007, according to the survey results. In response to a question about what would make school more engaging, teens not surprisingly said they would like to use personal laptops and mobile learning devices and would like to be able to take online classes and have access to technology tools while at school. More than half of them would like to see educational gaming become a part of school, noting that games make learning a complex concept more intriguing; consequently, they would "learn more" and "be more engaged." While teachers and administrators agree with students on the value of laptops, fewer than 20 percent of them agree with the teens on the value of educational gaming or the value of using mobile devices for learning. Teachers and administrators are even less supportive of using email and IM for learning. Parents, too, are half as likely as teens to advocate for online learning in today's schools.

The writers of the Project Tomorrow report referred to the differing perspectives between the digital natives and the digital immigrants as a *digital disconnect*. Is this digital disconnect partly to blame for the boredom among teens who drop out of school? Advocates for the use of emerging technologies for authentic learning situations in school would likely agree. Renowned researcher and visionary Seymour Papert (1993) put it this way: "Like any other social structure, School [sic] needs to be accepted by its participants. It will not survive very long beyond the time when children can no longer be persuaded to accord it a degree of legitimation" (p. 6).

What about the Digital Divide?

If we teach writing with the outside-of-school habits of digital natives in mind, are we leaving a child behind? A stream of literature about the so-called digital divide has recently flowed through professional publications, countless websites, the media, and state/national policy-making chambers. Since the construct was introduced in the mid-1990s, the field of education has become highly sensitive to the ways that access to all forms of technology is promoted or impeded based on culture, race, gender, and economic status. Even though, as some scholars argue, the meaning of a "digital divide" has never been quite clear (see Gunkel, 2003), we now have a much healthier knowledge base of what practices regarding technology in education are exclusionary, what programs and policies are not working, and who is being left out. And as a result, actions have been taken to narrow the divide. In addition, the ubiquity of technology has vastly increased over the last decade—computers, the Internet, cell phones, and other emerging technologies are becoming less expensive and more widely used. Consequently, what we mean by a "digital divide" may not be what we meant just two years ago when access to and ownership of technology were more limited. As Gunkel states, "Because the problems of the digital divide have been, and probably will continue to be, moving targets, the term's definition should be similarly mobile" (p. 505).

For many, the digital divide means unequal opportunities for particular populations to use digital tools. Recent studies show that we have moved rapidly toward closing the gap regarding equity and access, and economically underprivileged groups, in particular, are gaining ground. For instance, Greenhow (Nagel, n.d.) found that 77 percent of six hundred lower-income students surveyed have a profile on a social networking site such as MySpace or Facebook. Half of them use the Internet daily, and just over a quarter of them use it three to five times a week. Nearly all use the Internet, and 82 percent use it from a computer at home. We are not suggesting that inequities are fading away and our social blemishes are no longer staring us in the face. They still are. As Cummins, Brown, and Sayers (2007) note, this access-based view of the divide has been replaced by a pedagogical and cognitive divide. A pedagogical divide separates those students who receive information through top-down dissemination models of teaching from those students who engage in constructing information through meaningful inquiry. The cognitive divide describes how some use technology to drill and some use it for dialogue and discovery. Cummins and colleagues (2007) argue that current policy often forces marginalized students into "instructionally constricted learning environments" because they are viewed as having deficits that can be remediated with direct instruction. By limiting low-income and culturally diverse students to learning activities that use technology for remedial purposes—drill and practice—educators are marooning students. Consequently, low-income and culturally diverse students are the have-nots regarding engaging, inquiry-based technology-supported learning. This divide is arguably being fueled by curriculum and instruction that implement technology in engaging and creative ways for some but not all students.

We recognize inequities in how technology is integrated in lessons. We are also keenly aware of the potential danger of using online social platforms like Facebook, the potential for infringing on copyright law, and the facility with which students can plagiarize using the Web. Much has been written by scholars as well as the media about these and other red-flag concerns. We feel more light needs to be shed on what is good and what incredible projects digital natives and their teachers are doing, particularly projects that engage all students in meaningful writing activities. We are interested in what teachers like Josie and Adrienne in Texas are doing with their sixth graders. Josie's students design, write, and publish a literary magazine that is distributed to their community each spring. Adrienne's students, who are mostly Latino and low-income, engage in digital storytelling and produce poignant multimedia narratives about their lives. These are not exceptionally high-tech activities, but they do capture the interest of digital natives and they do create situations for multimodal writing and some use of the Web. Like so many schools, Josie's and Adrienne's schools limit how the Web can be used in school and prohibit the use of handheld devices like cell phones or iPods. Perhaps in the near future these teachers can more easily implement the tools and practices that digital natives use outside of school to enhance their teaching.

Our focus in this book is on how to use technology well when using it to write. Given the fact that students must know how to write to use the read-write Web and that they are already doing that prolifically outside of school, we feel it is important, if not urgent, that students in public, private, charter, and home schools write in all content areas and that teachers consider the interests, habits of mind, and demands facing these digital natives who will grow into their adult roles in a digital global society.

Frames Rather Than Stages in the Process

If textbooks used in secondary school English language arts classes since the 1980s were compared to textbooks used in the early 1960s, the most glaring difference might be that the more contemporary books have a notably dissimilar view of writing than the traditional perspective of early text-books. Research by Graves (1983), Emig (1983), Calkins (1986), and others on what writers do when they write triggered a movement, or paradigm shift, in how we see the recursive nature of stages in the writing process: prewriting, writing, revising, editing, and publishing. In many cases, text-books in the 1980s and 1990s explain the writing process as though it is a series of progressive steps. First prewrite. Then write. Then revise and edit. And finally, publish. Consequently, a secondary school curriculum typically has days or weeks dedicated to each "stage" of the process. In this book we neither support a perspective that views the writing process as a linear pro-gression of stages, nor do we see stages that can be cleanly defined and made absolutely distinct from each other. How each mind approaches the process of composing ideas and communicating them is highly individual, and par-ticularly, how technology complicates that endeavor forces us to rethink and question traditional ways of teaching the messy nature of "the process."

Rather than stages, procedures, or any other kind of format that sug-gests a step-by-step method of teaching writing with digital tools, we are proposing that four frames might better explain how the multitasking minds of digital natives approach the task of writing. The four frames are inside writing, responsive writing, purposeful writing, and social action writing. Certainly, these frames can be viewed in a linear way: first, in inside writing, the writer thinks about the topic and researches it; then, in responsive writing, the writer shares what she initially drafts with oth-ers; then, in purposeful writing, the writer revises and edits to be sure the audience for the piece will be satisfied and/or informed; and finally, in social action writing, the written piece is published with the intention of promoting change in the community. What happens when the writer trades the pen for an electronic tool that can connect the writer with the reader *throughout* the writing process, and when the writer can link a picture or a video to the writing? Exploring and researching (inside writing) can hap-pen at any point of the writing process, particularly when what is produced is in an interactive environment like a blog. Sharing writing (responsive writing) can happen all along the way, from start to finish, if the writer is working with others on a wiki. And although purposeful writing appears to be the frame that follows responsive writing, it may not occur only after collaborative writing is in some way finished. Students working in groups or alone might be in this frame of mind from the start of a project. That is, they might have determined that the purpose for their writing was to produce a podcast or a website, and they may have had an online audience in mind from the beginning. Specifically, we refer to revising and editing that is done at any point on words *and* on communicative forms other than words—images, animation, video, Web links, and so on. Given the electronic tools available, how a writer goes about answering the following questions takes on a different dimension than it has in the traditional sense: Is the product put together in a way that makes logical sense? Are the terms that are used precise enough? Are the ideas accurate? If the topic of the writing is something that relates to a local, national, or global issue (and we strongly feel that it should), inside writing, responsive writing, and purposeful writing will be frames of mind from which a digital native develops and expresses a stance. Writing to effect change based on that stance is social action writing.

The fluid, complex, and perhaps unwieldy nature of the process of writing is enhanced when words, music, animation, movies, and recorded voice add to a palette that previously only offered words and a canvas that only offered paper. Add to that the impact of interactivity that social networking on the Web and texting on cell phones has had on the act of exchanging ideas.

Given the changes in the way we communicate and given the habits of the digital natives, we recognize that we have outgrown the concept of the process of writing as a series of stages of manipulating words. When we explore the kaleidoscopic forms of individual and collaborative expression in the read-write Web world, we might go as far as to say that we have even outgrown the concept of recursive stages of writing. Then again, we might not go that far yet. How writing is defined and how it takes shape in this multidimensional and multimodal Web environment depends on the frame of mind of the writer.

Emphasis on Web 2.0

What, exactly, is the read-write Web, or Web 2.0? And why should schools make it available to students? Understanding the power of Web 2.0 means knowing what it is not. It is not Web 1.0, that online clickable world that we have "surfed" using our Internet browsers since the 1990s. That Web is static compared to Web 2.0. That is, although it is a powerful way to exchange information, images, sounds, and video clips because it links tens of thousands of computers across the world to provide a global information system, Web 1.0 is limited. Users can only view, listen to, or read what they find on this "information highway." There is some controversy surrounding the true definition of Web 2.0, but most generally agree that it is the technical iteration of the Web that has made it easy for anyone to add to its contents by simply clicking, keying-in, and uploading. It is social and participatory—users can as easily write in it as they can read it. Blogs, wikis, and podcasts are examples of Web 2.0 tools that are freely available to anyone who can get online. For some, that functionality holds the promise of opening channels for meaningful and instant dialogue among all people, not just among those who have the technical know-how to create a Web page. In fact, the Web 2.0 Summit, which started in 2004 and has been traditionally attended by technologists, announced that their conversation "is no longer just about the Web." The theme for its 2008 gathering focused on the users and not the architects of the Web:

> From harnessing collective intelligence to a bias toward open systems, the Web's greatest inventions are, at their core, social movements. To that end, we're expanding our program this year to include leaders in the fields of healthcare, genetics, finance, global business, and yes, even politics. (O'Reilly Media, 2008)

Hopefully, leaders in the field of education will join in this conversation as well. Educators can in many ways measure the pulse of the future. We are in very close contact with those digital natives who will be leading us and shaping our world—real and virtual. And those digital natives' habitat is the Web 2.0, the read-write Web. The implications for educators are starkly evident in the work of psychologists Lorin Anderson and David Krathwohl, students of Benjamin Bloom, developer of the well-known Bloom's Taxonomy, which has guided pedagogy since the 1950s (Bloom, 1956) (see Figure 1.1). Anderson updated the taxonomy in the 1990s to reflect what we know about how learners monitor their own thinking (Anderson & Krathwohl, 2001). Rather than knowledge, comprehension, application, analysis, synthesis, and evaluation, the new Bloom's Taxonomy lists remembering, understanding, applying, analyzing, evaluating, and creating (see Figure 1.2). Not only are the levels different, the static nouns of the 1950s

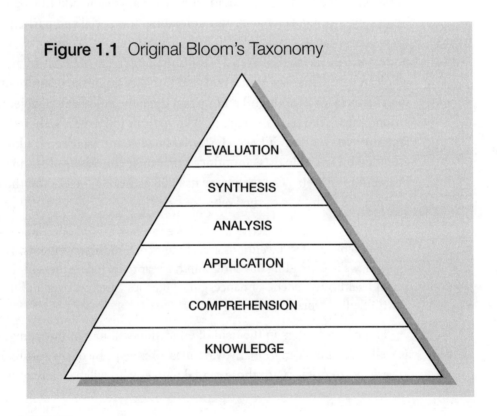

Figure 1.1 Original Bloom's Taxonomy

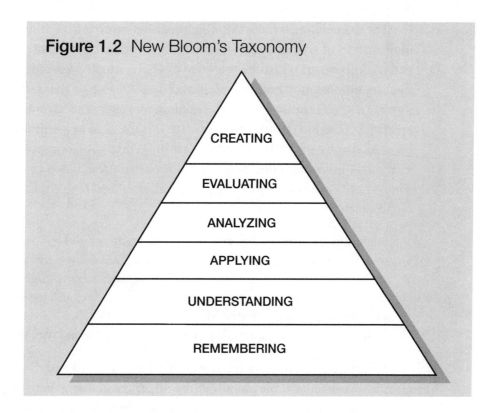

Figure 1.2 New Bloom's Taxonomy

CREATING

EVALUATING

ANALYZING

APPLYING

UNDERSTANDING

REMEMBERING

have been replaced with dynamic verbs—a subtle but significant modification, according to Cochran and Conklin (2007):

> Using verbs helps us focus on the behavior of the learner as opposed to the content of the material. It also does a better job of reflecting what Ralph Tyler recommended when he asked educators to look at a student's behavior at the end of an instructional sequence rather than focusing on the content of the lesson. Remembering, through processes such as recalling or recognizing, is a behavior that students can demonstrate at the end of a lesson and educators can use in their evaluations of student progress. In the new model we automatically look at what a learner will be able to do rather than the content or material to be learned. (p. 23)

The revised hierarchy of thinking processes evolved from a six-year-long analysis of studies on how we learn, and the changes reflect our current knowledge regarding the value of active, situated learning and metacognition, among other understandings. The impact that technology has had on how we access information, make sense of it, remix it, and create it is inherent in the new taxonomy. It is the kind of learning that will be needed as we move from the Information Age to the Conceptual Age, as Daniel Pink, in his popular book *A Whole New Mind* (2006), points out. Pink describes the Conceptual Age as one that values "high concept" and "high touch":

> High concept involves the capacity to detect patterns and opportunities, to create artistic and emotional beauty, to craft a satisfying narrative, and to combine seemingly unrelated ideas into something new. High touch involves the ability to empathize with others, to understand the subtleties of human interaction, to find joy in one's self and to elicit it in others, and to stretch beyond the quotidian in pursuit of purpose and meaning. (p. 52)

When a teacher imagines the vastness of information and the sea of people who are accessible literally at the fingertips of digital natives, possibilities are endless. When the teacher knows about the myriad of ways that these learners can interact through the read-write Web, opportunities for exciting, meaningful learning open up. And when the teacher thinks about how to prepare a young adult for the Conceptual Age, using tools for creating and for developing literacy is imperative. Wesley Fryer, in his blog "Moving at the Speed of Creativity" (n.d.), states that the greatest university of all is the content on and the people connected via the Internet:

> Today, I think literacy can be more accurately measured than ever before by not only the texts that are CONSUMED by learners, but rather by the authentic knowledge products they create (in a read/write context) as a result of their exposure to those ideas. We need to continually challenge the students in our care as well as our peers and ourselves to move beyond the knowledge/comprehension level of understanding, into the higher realms of analysis, synthesis, evaluation, and CREATION. When learners choose

to do those sorts of things on their own, and you see evidence of these types of thinking activities in their conversations, their blog posts, their blog comments, and their digital stories, then I think you can be confident the "educational process" is proceeding successfully for them.

Like Fryer, we feel confident that the use of Web 2.0, or the read-write Web, will become more and more prevalent in schools, and teachers and students will trade activities that relied on purchased software applications with activities that use no-cost online interactive participatory tools. And these activities will be organized in lessons that are built on the thinking processes described in the new Bloom's taxonomy. With that in mind and with the notion of four frames of writing, we will make over a lesson plan that is student centered, grounded in theory, and designed to address higher-order thinking. The make-over version of that lesson will include Web 2.0 tools and will be constructed so that it addresses the higher-order thinking skills of the 21st century.

What Is a Digital Make-Over of a Lesson?

The spark for this book came from our conversations with new teachers who had a wealth of knowledge about technology but a limited understanding of how to implement it in their instructional practices. We often thought that a back-door approach to professional development would work well with them. We think of this approach as mentoring or coaching. By looking at existing pedagogical practices, we could offer a make-over that would result in a revision of lessons so that instructional practices would be more in line with what digital natives know, like, and do. In this way, lessons could become more motivating for students. Rather than offering a new lesson plan, one that is partially or significantly different from what a teacher was already doing, we thought offering a make-over to an existing plan would be more easily accepted and implemented. Both the "good lesson" and the "make-over lesson" are presented in each chapter. The make-over lesson adds Web 2.0 tools, and consequently adds the real-world connection that can be made possible through writing and reading for/with a broad community. The lesson is realistic in that existing equipment could be used, regardless of most limitations such as number of computers available or quality of machines. It may be more idealistic in that it is designed for a school that will allow its students to access the Web, save information that is found there, and communicate online. We include a section that provides a window into the thoughts of digital natives we interviewed as they reviewed and tried the activities of the make-over lesson.

How to Read This Book

We are making assumptions about students, teachers, and curriculum in our explanation of the four frames of mind for writing in a digital age, and by making those assumptions explicit, we hope to make our message in each chapter understandable. Our assumptions are the following:

- *Students.* Many, if not most, secondary students are frequent users of technology. In particular, they use the social, participatory forms of online communication—IM, text messaging, social networking systems—and they use it primarily if not exclusively outside of school. Students are culturally diverse and some have special needs and are most often reading and writing in English at school.

- *Teachers.* Most secondary teachers are highly knowledgeable in their content areas and have a good to excellent understanding of appropriate and effective pedagogy. Some are proficient users of technology, and nearly all have access to at least one computer on their campuses. Most, if not all, schools have a technology coordinator, administrator, or lead teacher who is moderately to highly proficient with digital tools and who can assist teachers.

- *Curriculum.* Most secondary schools adhere to national standards for core content areas—English, math, social studies, and science. All schools/ districts provide professional development for teachers in at least one of these areas: differentiated instruction, assessment, reading/writing across the curriculum, technology.

In addition to these assumptions, we should emphasize that we are obviously advocates of writing across the curriculum, particularly in light of the ever-expanding use of the read-write Web. We also believe in the power of student-centered instruction, which can be associated with a constructivist theoretical orientation and such pedagogical methods as project-based learning, inquiry-based instruction, and authentic assessment. Each chapter focuses on one of the four frames and provides an example of how that frame plays out in a core subject area. Chapter 2, for example, explains inside writing and describes that frame through the remake of a ninth-grade social studies lesson on the Industrial Age. Chapter 3 explains collaborative writing and describes the remake of a seventh-grade science lesson on earth systems. In Chapter 4, purposeful writing is explained through the remake of an eighth-grade math lesson on measures of central tendency, and Chapter 5 focuses on social action writing and how it unfolds in a tenth-grade English lesson based on three well-known novels about social injustice. Each chapter could be read independently of others, but Chapters 3, 4, and 5 refer to the chapters before them in order to connect similar theoretical approaches, methods for instruction, and related concepts. We support our explanation of the frame and the lesson by describing a theoretical basis for it, and we incorporate a researched reading-writing strategy that is well known for its value for developing literacy in the content areas. Lesson plans are based on the lesson plan design outlined by Kellough and Kellough (2003). The context for the lesson, that is, the unit plan will be briefly described in order to situate the lesson within a larger instructional plan. We follow this section with a mini–case study of digital natives who did the activities described in the make-over lesson. At the end of each chapter, suggestions for how to adapt elements of the make-over in one content area are offered for other core content areas. We will also make a crucial connection that many teachers must consider in light of the growing diversity of our classrooms—effective instruction for English language learners (ELLs). For ELLs, we refer to the Sheltered Instruction Observation Protocol (SIOP) model (Echevarria, Vogt, & Short, 2008). It is important to note that the SIOP connections embedded in each lesson have proven to be effective strategies for many struggling students within a school's general population, regardless of language. Finally, Chapter 6 lists a number of resources and ideas to consider when doing a remake of a lesson.

Note that we will include Wikipedia in our lesson plans. Wikipedia is a nonprofit encyclopedia website, but unlike printed encyclopedias that are written and edited by a staff, Wikipedia is written and edited by anyone who can explore the Web. Authors and editors of information remain anonymous; consequently, information on Wikipedia is often considered questionable. Wikipedia creator Jimmy Wales, who was named by *Time* magazine as one of the "Top 100 People Who Shape Our World" (Anderson, 2006), envisioned a place where every person on the planet has free access to the sum of all human knowledge (Miller, 2004). Wikipedia was started in 2001 and has more than 2 million articles in English and articles written in more than 250 different languages. According to the traffic-monitoring service Hitwise, Wikipedia is one of the top ten sites on the Web, and it is consulted by more than a third of adults in the United States. Despite the controversy regarding its accuracy, it is more often frequented by the well educated than by those with lower levels of education. Its popularity and phenomenal growth is not reason enough to accept it as a reliable source of knowledge in classrooms, however. Wales himself admits that students sometimes use it in ways they should not. He stresses that its greatest value is that it has made information that was not readily available before accessible to anyone. We feel it is a good starting point when investigating a topic and agree with his advice: "Read Wikipedia for the background and then go out and do your own research. I mean, it's right there on the Internet, so your professors can look it up just like you did" (Mitchell, 2006).

It is critical to note that our make-over is not intended to be a lesson to pick up and apply directly, as would be the format of the recipe-type book we described at the start of this chapter. Rather, the lessons are meant to be models to demonstrate how any lesson can motivate digital natives to learn if it is intentionally designed and delivered with their interests and habits in mind. In summary, as you read this book, imagine the digital native as the central player in a virtual classroom that is not restricted to physical walls, is participatory, and can make learning and teaching an exciting and meaningful event.

Discussion Questions

1. Do you see yourself as an educator who is preparing students for the global culture and economy of the 21st century? Why or why not?

2. What are some of the behaviors/habits of the digital natives you have observed?

3. How might those behaviors/habits be channeled into educational activities that are suitable and beneficial for students?

References

Anderson, C. (2006). *Jimmy Wales.* Retrieved August 6, 2008, from www.time.com/time/magazine, April 30.

Anderson, L. W., & Krathwohl, D. R. (Eds.). (2001). *A taxonomy for learning, teaching, and assessing: A revision of Bloom's Taxonomy of Educational Objectives.* New York: Longman.

Atwell, N. (1987). *In the middle: Writing, reading, and learning with adolescents.* Portsmouth, NH: Heinemann.

Bloom, B. S. (1956). *Taxonomy of educational objectives, handbook 1: The cognitive domain.* New York: Longman.

Calkins, L. (1986). *The art of teaching writing.* Portsmouth, NH: Heinemann.

Cochran, D., & Conklin, J. (2007). A new Bloom: Transforming learning. *Learning & Leading with Technology, 34,* 22.

Cummins, J., Brown, K., & Sayers, D. (2007). *Literacy, technology, and diversity: Teaching for success in changing times.* Boston: Pearson/Allyn and Bacon.

Echevarria, J., Vogt, M. E., & Short, D. (2008). *Making content comprehensible for English learners: The SIOP Model* (3rd ed.). Boston: Pearson/Allyn and Bacon.

Emig, J. (1983). *The web of meaning.* Portsmouth, NH: Heinemann.

Fryer, W. (n.d.) *The greatest university of all.* Retrieved July 23, 2008, from www.speedofcreativity.org.

Graves, D. (1983). *Writing: Teachers and children at work*. Portsmouth, NH: Heinemann.

Gunkel, D. J. (2003). Second thoughts: Toward a critique of the digital divide. *New Media Society, 5,* 499–522.

Kellough, R. D., & Kellough, N. G. (2003). *Secondary school teaching* (2nd ed.). Upper Saddle River, NJ: Merrill/Prentice Hall.

Lawson, M. (2005). *Berners-Lee on the read/write web*. Retrieved August 2, 2008, from BBC website: http://news.bbc.co.uk/1/hi/technology/4132752.stm.

Lenhart, A., Arafah, S., Smith, A., & Macgill, A. R. (2008). *Pew Internet and American Life Project and the National Commission on Writing. Writing, Technology and Teens.* Retrieved July 22, 2008, from www.pewInternet.org.

Lenhart, A., Madden, M., Macgill, A. R., & Smith, A. (2007). *Pew Internet and American Life Project. Teens and Social Media.* Retrieved July 22, 2008, from www.pewinternet.org.

Miller, R. (2004). *Wikipedia founder Jimmy Wales responds*. Retrieved August 6, 2008, from http://interviews.slashdot.org, July 28.

Mitchell, R. (2006). *Wikipedi's creator: I'm not so influential*. Retrieved August 6, 2008, from www.sptimes.com/2006/06/18/Neighborhoodtimes, June 18.

Nagel, D. (n.d.). *Digital divide? What digital divide? T.H.E. Journal*. Retrieved June 23, 2008, from www.thejournal.com/articles/22818.

National Commission on Writing. (2004). *Writing: A ticket to work . . . Or a ticket out: A survey of business leaders*. Retrieved August 2, 2008, from www.writingcommission.org/pr/writing_for_employ.html.

O'Reilly Media, Inc. (2008). *Web 2.0 summit*. Retrieved August 2, 2008, from http://en.oreilly.com/web2008/public/content/home.

Papert, S. (1993). *The children's machine: Rethinking school in the age of the computer*. New York: Basic Books.

Pink, D. (2006). *A whole new mind*. New York: Penguin Group.

Prensky, M. (2006). *Don't bother me, mom, I'm learning*. St. Paul, MN: Paragon House.

Project Tomorrow. (2008). *21st century students deserve a 21st century education*. Retrieved July 22, 2008, from www.tomorrow.org.

The Silent Epidemic. (n.d.). Retrieved July 22, 2008, from www.silentepidemic.org.

Schoof, U. (2006). *Stimulating youth entrepreneurship: Barriers and incentives to enterprise start-ups by young people*. Geneva, Switzerland: International Labour Office.

Inside Writing

Key Elements in Chapter 2

Inside Writing The investigation of a topic using Web 2.0 tools. Inside writing is what a learner experiences as she begins to connect with text, images, sounds, animation, and so on.

Constructivism A theory about how we learn. The theory claims that we construct new knowledge as we interact with information and people. Constructivist class-rooms allow students to work in groups and monitor their learning.

KWL A strategy for helping students prepare to investigate a topic and monitor their own learning. K stands for *Know*; W stands for *Want* to know; and L stands for *Learned*.

Blog An online space designed for writing about any topic. Blogs are created by writers and are usually open for comments, or posts, from other reader/writers.

You should always start with your head and your heart.

Grant, grade 6

Chapter Preview

The launching point of the writing experience can be described as *inside writing*. In this frame, the adolescent writer who successfully enters into a writing project begins by becoming intrigued by a topic of interest. As new ideas are introduced, writers must have multiple opportunities to seek and gather new information in order to make the learning personally relevant and meaningful. Teachers can use many effective methods to help writers make personal connections with a topic they are exploring. Adding tech-nology, as in creating a multimedia folder, brings a new dimension to the learning experience. By actively engaging in online investigation and Web-based communication locally and globally, writers will begin to feel a sense of ownership of information and can claim a place in the classroom. This chapter will review schema theory, constructivism, and models of teaching writing and then describe the make-over of a social studies lesson on the Industrial Age to demonstrate what happens during inside writing.

What Is Inside Writing?

In the film *Finding Forrester* (Rich & Van Sant, 2000), actor Sean Connery plays William Forrester, a reclusive famous author, and Rob Brown plays Jamal, a highly talented African American college basketball star who struggles to find the confidence to unveil his true passion—writing. Connery's character advises Jamal: "You write your first draft with your heart and you rewrite with your head. The first key to writing is to write, not to think." At this point in the film, the young author is catapulted into a series of events that break down an imaginary barrier so that he discovers the confidence he needs for his talent to finally be realized. The metaphor of writing "with the heart" can be interpreted in any number of ways, one of which resonates with the mental frame we are calling **inside writing**. Inside writing might be best described as a process that addresses every student's need to become a part of the learning environment in order to participate fully in the act of communicating unique thoughts, of drawing conclusions, of developing arguments to persuade others, or of crafting artistic expressions. Before a student can become engaged in learning and using language purposefully and effectively, she must make personal connections with concepts in order to claim her place not only in the classroom but in the larger community that embraces the classroom. Inside writing from this perspective means that writers who are digital natives use technology to enhance personal connections.

Inside Writing
The investigation of a topic using Web 2.0 tools. Inside writing is what a learner experiences as she begins to connect with text, images, sounds, animation, and so on.

Why is making personal connections important? Before technology applications are considered for use in a classroom where students write to learn, consider the theory and philosophy underlying the reason why creating opportunities for students to make personal connections is so valuable. Making personal connections has long been recognized in educational psychology, in learning theory, and in the corresponding models for teaching.

Schema theory, for instance, emerged from the world of psychology in the early 1900s as an understanding of how we organize our perceptions of the world and how what we hold in memory shapes how we perceive new information. Research by schema theorists like Piaget (1929), Bartlett (1932), and Anderson (1984) illustrates how prior knowledge provides a mental framework that we use to make sense of new information. More recent research identifies how prior knowledge is culture-specific; consequently, schema theory is particularly useful to the identification of instructional models for second language learners (Carrell, Devine, & Eskey, 1988).

Teaching practices based on schema theory are built on the idea that students should learn broad and generic concepts in order to be able to make connections among specific ideas. For example, in a history class, a student needs to have prior knowledge of how power can be abused before understanding the reign of King George in England. To do that, a teacher might begin with a class discussion about power and how it is evident in students' lives. Using strategies designed to help create connections between their lives and global concepts, the teacher can guide the learners as they read about King George's rule and build their schema. Because difficulty in learning can be the result of insufficient schema, or a lack of prior knowledge, teachers can scaffold learning by using specific strategies designed to trigger prior knowledge, such as learning logs, videos, music, and role-playing. English language learners (ELLs), in particular, need support for drawing from their cultural knowledge as they learn English while at the same time learning new concepts in social studies, math, or science. Support for building schema can be provided through the use of specific reading strategies such as **KWL** (Ogle, 1986). This strategy prepares students for engaging in an exploration of information by asking them what they know (K), what they want to know (W), and what they have learned (L). By listing the knowledge they already have about a topic and posing their own questions to guide an investigation of that topic, students begin to take charge of their learning. In

KWL

A strategy for helping students prepare to investigate a topic and monitor their own learning. K stands for *Know*; W stands for *Want* to know; and L stands for *Learned*.

the example of a social studies lesson on King George's rule, students might be asked to list what they know about rulers—kings/queens, presidents, and other heads of state. They could then be asked what they know about King George, who was known as "the king who lost America." They would list questions triggered by curiosity, and by seeking answers to their own questions, they will begin to extend their understanding of rulers in general. This information can help them relate to how power was negotiated in England in the 1700s and how that led to the American Revolution. KWL and how it can be used with technology for investigations like this one will be discussed more fully in the lesson plan that explores inside writing.

How Does Constructivist Learning Theory Fit in Inside Writing?

The proponents of **constructivism** claim that by reflecting on personal experiences, learners construct their own understanding of the environment that surrounds them. Consequently, they make sense of the world by generating rules and mental models that serve as lenses from which they can begin to make sense of real *and* imagined experiences. (Living vicariously through a character while reading a novel is an example of an imagined experience.) In a constructivist view, learning is a search for meaning, and as new ideas are introduced in class, students must be given the opportunity to explore the issues from which they are actively trying to make meaning. In a constructivist classroom, then, learning happens as students gather information that makes the new ideas relevant and meaningful to their lives. The teacher assists in this effort, collaborating with students in their search for how information connects with their lives. In the example of the students who are studying King George's reign, a constructivist approach for learning means that students would

Constructivism
A theory about how we learn. The theory claims that we construct new knowledge as we interact with information and people. Constructivist classrooms allow students to work in groups and monitor their learning.

be provided multiple forms of information and various opportunities for dialogue. They would be encouraged to explore by investigating what power means in their lives and building their own theories about how power shapes communities. Writing about their discoveries and their theories engages students in a process of defining or constructing their knowledge of the world.

Jacqueline Grennon Brooks (2004) describes the constructivist roles of students and teachers succinctly:

> Constructing knowledge talks about how we as the learners are reformulating, refiltering, relooking at constantly the way that we see our world, that the teacher can't give away explanations, the teacher can't give away knowledge, the student can't receive it passively from the teacher. The learning and teaching dynamic is a process of negotiation in which the people come to the table, try to make sense of the world, and in any one particular instance try to make sense of the concept at hand.

Inside writing is what happens in a constructivist classroom connected to the world via the Web. The computer does not reshape how writing is taught. Writing in a constructivist classroom, as all learning activities in this kind of environment, is based on a perspective of the learner as self-monitoring but guided by a knowledgeable adult. This can happen with or without a computer. However, the computer opens avenues for exploring. By adding access to online resources in this setting, teachers can create opportunities for students to greatly intensify the learning experience. The act of writing, when it occurs in what we call inside writing, is inherently constructivist. To clarify, we need to first examine how writing has traditionally been taught with limited or no use of the computer.

Models of teaching writing have an even longer history than theories about how we learn. Many of today's methods for teaching writing, for instance, have roots in the ancient Greek philosophers and Roman rhetoricians who mastered the technique of composition and the art of teaching it. In contemporary times, the notion of a *process* of writing has been widely accepted as the starting place for building daily lessons on writing. Janet Emig (1971) may be one of the most frequently cited scholars in publications and conversations about how the view of writing as a process began.

Her study of twelfth-grade writers revealed that writers engage in a variety of cognitive activities as they write—planning, drafting, writing, revising, and rewriting. Just prior to the Emig study, participants at the renowned 1966 Dartmouth Seminar, a gathering of American and British college English faculty, ended with a rousing declaration that writing should be taught altogether differently. At the time, the typical writing assignment was made on one day, the paper was collected a few days later, and the graded paper—typically marked with red corrections—reflected an evaluation of a final product with no review or evaluation of drafts along the way. In the three decades that followed, "process writing" became as well-known and practiced in English classes to guide the production of a final draft as formulas are learned and applied in math classes to arrive at solutions to problems. In the 1990s, the tenets of process writing were challenged by those who viewed the method as too structured to capture the *act* of writing. Proponents of post–process writing argue that the act of writing is, in fact, the act of making sense and that writing is how we interpret our world. Consequently, it cannot be "reduced to a generalizable process" (Kent, 1999, p. 5).

Whether writing and the teaching of writing are explored through the lens of educational psychology, learning theory, process writing, or post–process writing, writing is primarily a physical act that begins with a cognitive, emotional, or social connection to the writer's world. Those connections are not only recognized by the writer, they are acted on, even modified through the process of composing, which until just a few years ago was done primarily with pencil, pen, or typewriter and printed on a paper-based medium. We have moved into what David Reinking and colleagues (1998) call a "post-typographic" society. Given the tools we have for writing today, those compositions may include text, graphics, animation, or sound. The digital natives described in Chapter 1 are, in fact, naturally inclined to compose in this way. Inside writing for them means making connections via the electronic tools they use to find information, to make sense of the world, and to construct knowledge for themselves. To demonstrate how a good inside writing lesson can be transformed into one that keeps in mind the digital native, we will follow Anna, a fictional but typical ninth grader, as she engages in learning about and defining the Industrial Age in a social studies class.

What Is a Good
Inside Writing Lesson?

Anna's social studies class teacher begins a unit on the Industrial Age by instructing his students to write a response to this statement: "Even in the 21st century, there are some countries that have not experienced an Industrial Revolution." For Anna and her classmates, who are likely unfamiliar, and perhaps unconcerned, with a time called the Industrial Age, this may be an intriguing but confusing statement. Anna's teacher believes in a constructivist philosophy and recognizes the value of guiding his students to a deeper understanding of their own lives by exploring the lives of people in past generations whose actions shaped today's world. For adolescents, imagining how historical events can have any bearing on their daily lives can be difficult. To trigger prior knowledge so that students can begin to make a connection with the topic, the teacher will use the KWL strategy—an approach that will help students define and understand what is meant by the term *Industrial Age*.

The KWL lesson that follows would occur over one or two days and would introduce a unit of study that extends over two or more weeks and follows units that focus on other time periods in American history. A number of classroom activities will help students make sense of information regarding the Industrial Age. Along the way, students will consider how today's Digital Age is similar to and different from the Industrial Age. They will also identify aspects of today's society that are a result of actions taken during the Industrial Age. Lessons that follow this one will guide students to the next writing steps. That is, students would use the information they gathered during this lesson to write any of the following: a summary of one topic, theme, or issue of the time period; a biography of a person who influenced change; a position paper on the positive or negative influence of that period on society; or a news report of an event or series of events of the time. This lesson, then, is the beginning of the writing experience in the unit.

Know, Want to Know, Learned (KWL) Lesson Plan

Materials

- newspaper clippings—historical and contemporary articles about Industrial Revolutions

- magazines—historical and contemporary articles about Industrial Revolutions

- textbook

- books from library about U.S. labor unions, women's suffrage movement, immigration, child labor, health and sanitation, life in the mines and factories, textile mill conditions, technology and scientific advances

Goal

Students understand what defines and characterizes the Industrial Age and how that relates to today's Digital Age.

Rationale

The progression of a society is essentially dependent on economic and political forces, advances in science and engineering, and demographic/cultural changes. Learning about the American Industrial Age will help students situate themselves in time and location so that they understand local and global forces that are currently influencing them.

Curriculum Standard (from National Council for the Social Studies)

Thematic Strand II: Time, Continuity, and Change

- Social studies programs should include experiences that provide for the study of the ways human beings view themselves in and over time, so that the learner can:

  - identify and describe significant historical periods and patterns of change within and across cultures, such as the development of ancient cultures and civilizations, the rise of nation-states, and social, economic, and political revolutions.

Know, Want to Know, Learned (KWL) Lesson Plan (cont'd)

Objectives

- Students will describe what they know about the Industrial Age.

- Students will suggest questions regarding the Industrial Age.

- Using teacher-provided materials, students will summarize information that answers the questions they posed.

Activities

- Introduction: Write this statement on the board: "Even in the 21st century, there are some countries that have not experienced an Industrial Revolution." Ask students to silently consider what the statement might mean.

- Activity 1: Below the statement, draw a 3-column table, the first column headed by the letter *K*. Ask students what they *know* about the statement. Under the K, list what students *know*.

- Activity 2: Under the second column, write "W." List what students want to know about the statement. Write these in a question format.

- Activity 3: Distribute materials (newspaper clippings, magazines, books, etc.) and ask students to read through these and their textbook to find answers for the questions they posed in the W column.

- Activity 4: Under the third column, write "L." List information the students have *learned* after reading materials. Ask students if they have other questions to add to the W column and ask what sources could be used to find more information.

- Closure: Bring students' attention to the statement presented in the introduction. Ask them to share their thoughts regarding the statement.

Know, Want to Know, Learned (KWL) Lesson Plan (cont'd)

Modifications

Embedded in this lesson are recognized practices for addressing diversity, that is, relating to life experience, providing group support, using project-centered learning, and creating a structured learning environment. English as a second language (ESL) students' learning can be further reinforced through the use of materials printed in their native languages and books that have effective illustrations.

Assessment

Formative assessment of quality of questions and responses to the questions

---

How Is a Good Inside Writing Lesson Made Better?

The KWL lesson plan will enhance students' schema and demonstrate a constructivist approach to learning. It can be improved, however, when it is reimagined with the digital native in mind. This social studies teacher is a facilitator, but his role is limited by the availability of materials from which his students can gather new information and construct knowledge. For today's technology-savvy students, researching digital sources to make meaning of new terms and concepts may be more engaging than sifting through printed materials the teacher provides or that are available in the classroom/library. With the use of technology, the walls of the school dissolve and a vibrant, dynamic environment emerges—one that allows students to investigate online resources and exchange ideas with people outside the classroom. Enhancing the KWL lesson's activities to include the vast body of information available online will expand students' opportunities for learning in many ways. Instead of being limited to what is delivered in text-books and other print materials, students can experience sound, video, and animation. Imagine watching an early 1900s scratchy sepia-toned moving picture documenting what life was like during the Industrial Revolution (see www.teachertube.com and www.howstuffworks.com) or perusing count-less maps, documents, and films of the early 1900s stored at the Library of Congress in Washington (see www.loc.gov). Given the facility or, some may say, the unwieldy awkwardness by which all of this information can be navi-gated, the idea of providing digital pathways for students to make connec-tions is well warranted. For this reason the teacher's role is more important than ever. Rather than being the facilitator who organizes information and guides learning, Anna's teacher is more like the captain of a crew on a learn-ing journey. The starting point of the online journey is inside writing.

To help students like Anna as they engage in inside writing activities, teachers might first consider the kinds of thinking students are doing. They are exploring, investigating, gathering information, brainstorming, orga-nizing, and synthesizing. They may use a variety of technological tools but are most likely to use Web tools not only to explore, investigate, and gather information, but to experience it as well through video and sound. After searching through sites for information about the Industrial Age, students could collect information in an online database (see Google Base), a mind mapping program (see www.mindmeister.com), or a wiki (see www.pbwiki .com). The possibilities for electronic tools can be overwhelming for teach-ers, so the best way to start may be to think of how digital natives explore and investigate and then consider the tools.

Exploring and Investigating Digitally

A popular starting point for most information gatherers in Anna's posi-tion is a Google search that begins with the predictable task of typing in *Industrial Age*. Anna could also begin her search with Wikipedia. The definition of Industrial Age may change frequently on Wikipedia because political events of the day or new perspectives on historical events may inspire users to edit what is posted. Anna may or may not know how democratic and changeable the information she found is, but she knows that she can find nearly any topic there, in a language other than English if needed, and that she too can modify it with new or different information, if she chooses to do so. She may float around other sites on the Web to examine photos, graphics, video, and primary documents such as those made available through the Library of Congress site. Or, she may engage in a conversation on a **blog** that focuses on the topic. As she is viewing and possibly adding to or revising a website she has located, she is constructing her own knowledge of the Industrial Age and participating in a global online conversation about the topic. Until the read-write Web became available, students could not conceive of constructing knowledge in this way—with five or five thousand people—in just about any language. Inside writing is the first engagement in the activity that will culminate in a product or project that communicates Anna's newly acquired understanding of the Industrial Age, a skill that is essential today. As David Warlick (2007) states, "As little as we know about the future for which we are preparing our students, it is clear that it will be a place that is governed by information. Accessing, processing, building with, and communicating that information is how we will all make our livings."

Blog
An online space designed for writing about any topic. Blogs are created by writers and are usually open for comments, or posts, from other reader/writers.

What Is a Good Digital Version of an Inside Writing Lesson?

The following lesson is a remake of the KWL lesson. It still uses KWL as the strategy and has an identical goal and rationale, and objectives are similar. The activities and materials, however, are significantly different.

KWL Lesson Plan—The ReMake

Materials

- computers with Internet access, projector

- blog

- Inspiration or other freeware conceptual organizer like FreeMind.

- TeacherTube video: "If I Had a Million Dollars" (found at www.teachertube .com/ view_video.php?viewkey=0731cb31eb6e9bcf7967)

- textbook

- suggested list of topics for online search: U.S. labor unions, women's suffrage movement, immigration, child labor, health and sanitation, life in the mines and factories, textile mill conditions, technology and scientific advances

- suggested English websites: www.loc.gov (Library of Congress), www.kidinfo.com, www.encarta.msn.com

- suggested Spanish websites: www.laguia2000.com, www.artehistoria.jcyl.es, www.telemundo.yahoo.com, www.wikilearning.com

Goal

Students understand what defines and characterizes the Industrial Age and how that relates to today's Digital Age.

Rationale

The progression of a society is essentially dependent on economic and political forces, advances in science and engineering, and demographic/cultural changes. Learning about the American Industrial Age will help students situate themselves in time and location so that they understand local and global forces that are currently influencing them.

KWL Lesson Plan—The ReMake (cont'd)

Curriculum Standard (from National Council for the Social Studies)

Thematic Strand II: Time, Continuity, and Change

■ Social studies programs should include experiences that provide for the study of the ways human beings view themselves in and over time, so that the learner can:

● identify and describe significant historical periods and patterns of change within and across cultures, such as the development of ancient cultures and civilizations, the rise of nation-states, and social, economic, and political revolutions.

Objectives

■ Students will describe what they know about the Industrial Age.

■ Students will suggest questions regarding the Industrial Age.

■ Using the Web, students will summarize information that answers the questions they posed.

Activities

■ Introduction: Show the TeacherTube video "If I Had a Million Dollars" (see Materials list) or a similar video. On the board, write: "Even in the 21st century, there are some countries that have not experienced an industrial revolution." Ask students to silently consider what the statement might mean.

■ Activity 1: Use Inspiration or a similar freeware program to brainstorm what students know. Type "Industrial Age" in the center symbol. Create two symbols connected to the center one. Label one "K." Ask students what they *know* about the statement. In the K symbol, use the brainstorm tool to list what students *know*.

■ Activity 2: Label the second symbol "W." Within that symbol list what students *want* to know about the statement. Use the brainstorm tool to write questions students want answered.

KWL Lesson Plan—The ReMake (cont'd)

- Activity 3: Ask students to gather in pairs around computers in the room/lab and use tools such as Google, Yahoo, or Wikipedia to explore ideas listed in the questions in the W symbol.

- Activity 4: As students are finding information (text, photos, graphics, and/or video), they will post it on the class blog named The American Industrial Age—What We *Learned*.

- Closure: Bring students' attention to the statement presented in the introduction. Ask them to share their thoughts regarding the statement. Project the blog using the computer and a digital projector, and randomly select posts to read. Remind students to post other questions and their answers in the class blog.

Modifications

As in the original lesson, the remake is built on the recognized practices for addressing diversity that were listed earlier. In addition, providing a list of websites in Spanish and showing students how to find articles in Spanish and other languages in Wikipedia will be helpful for ELLs. Encourage them to focus on the links for other websites within the Wikipedia article.

Assessment

Formative assessment of quality of questions and responses to the questions and comments on class blog

---

After students are introduced to the topic in this lesson, the inside writing that has begun will lead to other forms of writing/thinking. For instance, the inside writing lesson could set the stage for discussion about China and India and how those emerging industrial powers compare to or influence the United States. By identifying differences between an industrialized nation and one that is not or one that is becoming one, students will be able to draw conclusions about advantages or disadvantages of industrialization. Remember the discussion about schema theory and constructivism and consider how exploring the Web for information triggers prior knowledge, builds on it, and promotes the construction of new knowledge based on the experience of connecting to the world in meaningful ways. One of these meaningful ways may be viewing and capturing photos and reading text from websites that can help students understand the impact of industrialization in general. The website www.chinatoday.com, for instance, will give Anna information about the "second industrial revolution" as it refers to the dramatic transformation China is experiencing. She may wonder about her future after she learns about global economic developments and explores a site like U.S. Department of Labor's Jobs for the 21st century to learn more about what matters to her and her peers: a successful future.

Imagine how Anna might maneuver through sites like these. As she's reading text, viewing photos, and listening to sound files, she's sorting through information to find those pieces that are meaningful to her. She can then gather photos, text, and sound files and save them in a multimedia folder for later use as she might have done when she took notes in a traditional paper-based journal, log, or notebook. She can also share and critique her understandings with her classroom community through the class blog. Here she is invited to post her comments and by doing this, to claim a place in the classroom as someone who is informed and has a voice. Creating a blog using a tool like www.blogger.com, for instance, will provide Anna and peers an opportunity to express themselves and claim a place in the larger community. And these students can do more. Suppose that Anna is most fascinated by the issue of technology in industrialized and nonindustrialized countries. By creating her own blog on this topic, she will connect digitally with others to explore how her generation is experiencing a move from an Industrial Age to a Digital Age. What does this mean for her? What does it mean for adolescents in advanced countries like the United States, European countries, and in rapidly advancing countries like China? What does it mean for adolescents in the Middle East, in Africa, and in developing, or third-world, countries? She can ask what this means for her future and begin to use the thinking processes we are associating with inside writing: exploring, investigating, gathering information, brainstorming, organizing, and synthesizing. As Anna engages in these processes, she is connecting with the world and composing her message about her interpretations of what she is learning.

Anna and her classmates' engagement in inside writing could certainly have occurred in the first KWL lesson we described, but perhaps with important limitations. The personal connections she made with the various levels of community could only be achieved with the access that technology provides. Most important, in the lesson remake, Anna learned in a way that fits her digital native habits.

How Do We Know
That Anna Is Learning?

It is not unreasonable for a teacher to feel apprehensive when he moves his classroom beyond the security of four walls and into the digital world. He might wonder if the natives will follow the course that has been charted for them and if they will gather information that is relevant to the learning objective. It is interesting to note that these are valid concerns in any classroom, traditional or digital. But the teacher who leads his students out into the digital world will become a guide and a collaborator, two roles the natives recognize and value, and if our interviews are any indication, the journey into the digital unknown will be extraordinary.

What should a teacher expect to see when the natives travel into their digital world? According to the digital natives we interviewed, the classroom environment and the work that follows depends on who the work is for. If the teacher limits the exploring and information gathering to a predetermined list of search topics—for example, Industrial Age or Industrial Revolution—the natives will probably conduct their initial searches using a strategy they call "random clicking," and they are unlikely to move beyond page one of the search results. If, however, the students are encouraged to begin with Industrial Age and then guided to follow their own leads, to drill down into areas of personal interest, as they are in a KWL lesson, the work takes on a whole new meaning.

According to Harley, a fourteen-year-old, "I just click on random stuff if it's for the teacher, and I stay on the first page. The teacher just wants information, and I can find lots of that on the first page."

John, a thirteen-year-old, also sees random clicking as the first step in exploring a new topic on the Web. When asked to gather information about the Industrial Age, John conducted his first search in Google and clicked on topics such as "definition of the Industrial Age" and "inventors of the Industrial Age." When he did not find information that interested or inspired him, John traveled to Wikipedia. While there, he clicked on maps and drilled down to information about nonindustrialized nations. For John, his search became an information gathering session about the politics of nonindustrialized nations because, as John sees it, "It's usually the government that keeps a country from developing."

John's search did not end there. He clicked on a link to Haiti because ". . . it's one of the least developed nations, and it's close to the United States." Within minutes, John found information that was relevant to him, and more important, he found his place in the classroom.

When given the freedom to drill for his own information, Harley was able to find his place in the classroom, too. "If I'm looking for facts about specific things, like if I already know something about the topic, I narrow my search—Industrial Age and cars. I like cars, and I know cars were a big part of the Industrial Age, so I'd narrow my search. I'd start looking at Model Ts."

After the information is gathered, the teacher will probably wish for some form of tangible proof that their day in the computer lab was productive, and the natives will not fail him. It is an interesting phenomenon that the digital natives, in addition to their streamlined, personalized ways of gathering information, have a natural tendency to deposit the information they have gathered into some form of personalized text.

John, for example, prefers to move his relevant information into a Word document. "I put my information in Word or Publisher. I copy and paste a lot of information on one page. I take out all the boring stuff and print it. Pictures, too. I make my own book."

Harley chooses to move his information into a personalized digital journal. "I paste a lot of information on one page. I keep it—get good facts from lots of good sites and keep it. I don't need to print it out. I just save it."

Just like their immigrant counterparts, the natives appear to be gatherers and keepers of information. The teacher in a digital classroom, however, should realize that while a majority of students from 20th century classrooms were willing to absorb and repeat information that was given to them, the natives of the 21st century are in search of information that is relevant to them and that connects them to a larger, global learning community. Because of technology, they are part of a worldwide classroom. They exchange ideas, they share insights and knowledge, and they sift through enormous reserves of good and bad information to find what is most meaningful and true to them.

While we are focused on gathering, storing, and sharing information found on the Web, it is important to address an issue that affects teachers and students in all content areas—copyright law and fair use guidelines for the classroom. Undoubtedly, teachers understand the importance of properly citing sources and giving credit to the originators/creators of text, images, videos, podcasts, and other resources. Teachers are also mindful of the restrictions placed on copyrighted materials—ranging from traditional books to DVDs to software—that they use regularly in their classrooms. But in this age of information at our fingertips, it is imperative that students, too, understand the policies (nationally and locally) regarding the use of information and resources found on the web. As students begin to search the Web, it will be beneficial for the teacher and students to discuss copyright law and fair use guidelines and to establish procedures for properly using and citing text, images, video files, and audio files gathered during activities such as KWL. There are many websites that teachers may refer to as they guide students through the complexities of copyright law.

Students who learn to follow copyright law as they engage in online learning are also learning to be responsible consumers of information in the Digital Age—an age in which individuals are eager to share their intellect and creativity with a global audience. It is in our best interest to teach our students to be conscientious gatherers and users of a global collection of knowledge.

For Harley and John, two gatherers who benefited from the contributions of a global community, the Industrial Age is now more than a topic that the teacher writes on the board. For Harley, it is an opportunity to learn about the advent of the automobile and to possibly track the auto industry's beginning to the fuel-dependent nation we are today. He might even begin to make connections between fuel consumption and global warming. For John, this new topic is the beginning of exploring nonindustrialized nations and thinking critically about how a government can determine the economic well-being of its people. For both boys, they are now connected to the new learning. They have become part of the learning environment, and they have started with what matters most—head and heart. For Harley and John's teacher, his classroom has moved beyond the traditional four walls. He is a guide and collaborator as his students engage in *inside writing*.

Chapter Summary

Inside writing occurs at the beginning of an investigation of a topic. Prior knowledge can be triggered by the use of strategies designed to help students know what they already know and how they will seek new, meaningful information. The KWL strategy is an effective one for that purpose and a strategy that can be enhanced with technology. For digital natives, using technology is a natural way to explore what they know and for finding and processing new information. Online searches provide vast and unique sources of knowledge—text, graphics, sound, and video can be examined and collected. Interactive Web 2.0 tools like wikis and blogs allow opportunities for person-to-person exchanges that help students construct knowledge as well as make claims about what they know. By forming notions about a concept in this manner, these digital natives are becoming more empowered and consequently more confident in their expertise. They can take a stance on a topic and establish voice in their writing as they express themselves with authority in the next frame of the writing experience: responsive writing.

Inside Writing Practice in Science, Math, and English Language Arts

To practice ways of remaking a lesson plan so that it addresses inside writing, use the sample social studies remake lesson as a guide to design a plan that uses KWL in science, math, or English language arts.

Science: In science class, students can focus on the scientists and inventors of the Industrial Age and their contributions. Consider what students should know about people like Richard Arkwright, Alexander Graham Bell, Henry Bessemer, Thomas Alva Edison, Samuel Morse, Louis Pasteur, James Watt, and Eli Whitney in order to understand the impact of science on society. Think of ways to guide students to an understanding of how today's scientists are affecting how adolescents live and how they will live as young adults. Keep in mind the tools on Web 2.0, online databases, Inspiration, and other resources as you plan the lesson.

Address this content standard from the National Council of Teachers of Science:

- As a result of activities in grades nine through twelve, all students should develop understanding of science as a human endeavor, the nature of science, and the history of science.

  - Individuals and teams have contributed and will continue to contribute to the scientific enterprise.

Math: A math lesson focused on gathering statistical data can be anchored in a study of the Industrial Age. Applying mathematical skills to content of interest to the students will strengthen their skills. Have students use online tools for finding the historical numbers they will need. Design a KWL-based lesson to guide students as they consider using statistical computations to make sense of trends in the Industrial Age such as the number of people moving from rural areas to the city, the number of cars produced over time, the numbers and origins of immigrants arriving at Ellis Island, and so forth. InspireData is a very powerful tool for gathering numerical information—consider having students use that as they gather, organize, and synthesize what they find.

Address this content standard from the National Council of Teachers of Mathematics:

- Mathematics instructional programs should include attention to data analysis, statistics, and probability so that all students pose questions and collect, organize, and represent data to answer those questions.

English Language Arts: *The Great Gatsby* (Fitzgerald, 1925) can be the literature study that helps students make sense of how culture and society, particularly as they are interpreted in the Industrial Age mentality of the 1920s, shape our collective worldview. Students can explore the book's theme, characters, setting, and Fitzgerald's use of symbol to make sense of social classes, cultural and gender-based privilege and access, the American dream, and corruption. They can also read contemporary young adult literature set in the Industrial Revolution time period—books by Avi, Scott O'Dell, Katherine Paterson, and Linda Holeman. Design a KWL lesson plan that leads students to Web searches to find connections the author makes with the novel's setting to explore the societal and economic divisions. Consider having students use blogs to overlay their ideas on issues of the Digital Age and the American Dream.

Address these content standards from the National Council of Teachers of English:

- Students read a wide range of literature from many periods in many genres to build an understanding of the many dimensions (e.g., philosophical, ethical, and aesthetic) of human experience;

- Students use a variety of technological and information resources (e.g., libraries, databases, computer networks, and video) to gather and synthesize information and to create and communicate knowledge.

Table 2.1 Resources for Inside Writing

Inside Writing Thinking Processes	Web Links and Tools Used in Social Studies ReMake Lesson
Exploring	www.wikipedia.com 　　online encyclopedia www.google.com 　　search engine
Investigating	www.askjeeves.com http://wiki.answers.com/ 　　online information-finding tools
Gathering data	www.libraryofcongress.gov 　　primary resources www.bls.gov/opub/working/home.htm 　　information about 21st century jobs
Brainstorming	MS Word Inspiration 　　software for word processing and mind mapping
Organizing	MS Word Inspiration 　　software for word processing and mind mapping
Defining/Redefining	www.blogger.com www.wordpress.com 　　online interactive journals (blogs)

Sites to learn more about Copyright and Fair Use Law:

http://home.earthlink.net/~cnew/research.htm

www.education-world.com/a_curr/curr280.shtml

www.utsystem.edu/ogc/intellectualproperty/copypol2.htm

Discussion Questions

1. How can the remake lesson described in this chapter be modified to fit in your classroom and to meet the needs of your students? If you are not teaching yet, consider how the remake lesson could be modified to fit a classroom you have observed.

2. What may be some of the obstacles and challenges involved in implementing a technology-rich lesson?

3. How can these possible obstacles and challenges be overcome?

4. What is an effective lesson that can be made better by using the KWL strategy and technology?

References

Anderson, R. C. (1984). The notion of schemata and the educational enterprise: General discussion of the conference. In R. C. Anderson, R. J. Spiro, & W. E. Montague (Eds.), *Schooling and the acquisition of knowledge.* Hillsdale, NJ: Lawrence Erlbaum.

Bartlett, F. C. (1932). *Remembering: An experimental and social study.* Cambridge: Cambridge University Press.

Brooks, J. G. (2004). Constructivism as a paradigm for teaching and learning. Retrieved April 6, 2008, from www.thirteen.org/edonline/concept2class/constructivism/demonstration.html.

Carrell, P. L., Devine, J., & Eskey, D. E. (1988). *Interactive approaches to second language reading.* Cambridge: Cambridge University Press.

Emig, Janet. (1971). *The composing process of twelfth graders.* Research Report No. 13. Urbana, IL: NCTE.

Fitzgerald, F. S. (1925). *The great Gatsby.* New York: Scribner's.

Kent, T. (1999). Introduction. In T. Kent (Ed.), *Post–process theory: Beyond the writing process paradigm* (pp. 1–6). Carbondale: Southern Illinois University Press.

Miller, T. L. (Writer). (n.d.). *If I had a million dollars.* [film] USA. Retrieved March 22, 2008, from www.teachertube.com/view_video.php?viewkey=0731cb31eb6e9bcf7967.

Ogle, D. S. (1986). K-W-L group instructional strategy. In A. S. Palincsar, D. S. Ogle, B. F. Jones, & E. G. Carr (Eds.), *Teaching reading as thinking* (pp. 11–17). Alexandria, VA: Association for Supervision and Curriculum Development.

Piaget, J. (1929). *The child's conception of the world.* New York: Harcourt, Brace Jovanovich.

Reinking, D., McKenna, M. C., Labbo, L. D., & Kieffer, R. D. (1998). *Handbook of literacy and technology: Transformations in a post-typographic world.* Hillsdale, NJ: Erlbaum.

Rich, M. (Writer), & Van Sant, G. (Director). (2000). *Finding Forrester* [Motion picture]. USA: Columbia Pictures Corporation.

Warlick, D. (2007). 21st century literacy for school boards of education. Retrieved August 7, 2008, from http://davidwarlick.com/wiki/pmwiki.php/Main/HomePage, October 4.

Responsive Writing

Key Elements in Chapter 3

Responsive Writing Students work in groups that communicate in person as easily as they do online through the use of blogs, wikis, and course management systems. They may also use online tools to collaboratively write with people beyond their school and community.

Collaborative Learning Collaborative learning in a responsive writing frame is the lively interaction that occurs when minds are in the act of inquiry, of discovery, of making sense of a construct by attempting to define or label it. It is a process that involves questioning, challenging, and validating the ideas written by each member of the group.

Group Mapping Activity (GMA) The Group Mapping Activity is a strategy designed to help students make sense of information. By using concept maps created on paper and/or online, students arrange information in ways that depict the meaning of terms and concepts and the connections between and among them.

Wiki Like blogs, wikis are online spaces for writing and posting. A wiki allows writers to work on one document that is stored online and can be accessed through the Internet. Wikis also allow students to store pictures, graphics, movies, and other objects.

Here's a little chunk of my life, and now I understand it better.

Leigh, grade 9

Chapter Preview

The frame of writing that extends the inside writing experience is *responsive writing*. In this frame, adolescent writers share and reconstruct their knowledge by interacting with each other in small response groups. These response groups serve as a forum for students to test theories, rethink those theories, and label emerging ideas. By labeling, students use language to make sense of new concepts, skills, and problem-solving strategies. Their understandings are tested when their conclusions are examined by others, and by examining and evaluating conclusions, students broaden their own knowledge and develop open-mindedness. This chapter will discuss what we know about collaborative learning and how models of inquiry apply in responsive writing. We will then describe how the make-over of a science lesson that focuses on a comparison of global warming[1] and the Dust Bowl is enhanced through the use of technology-supported responsive writing.

What Is Responsive Writing?

Apollo 13 (Grazer, 1995), the movie directed by Ron Howard in 1995, is not only a study of one of NASA's near tragedies in its efforts to gain scientific knowledge of our universe, it is also a study of intense purposeful collaboration. When three astronauts are trapped in a disabled capsule on its return from a failed moon exploration mission in 1970, the Houston-based mission control team scrambled desperately to find a way to safely guide the marooned astronauts through the 205,000-mile journey home. In one scene, a small group of engineers gathers materials that are available to the astronauts so that they can restore the failing oxygen system. The engineers begin to work with this odd collection, each time trying a new combination and talking about what will and will not work. Eventually, they emerge from their laboratory with instructions for the stranded astronauts on how to use things like a sock, duct tape, and plastic bags to repair the capsule well enough to be able to maintain the life support system they will need as they maneuver the crippled craft home.

In a similar spirit of collaboration that existed among these scientists, collaboration among writers leads to finding just the right language to

---

[1]According to the National Academy of Sciences, *global warming* is an average increase in the temperature of the atmosphere near the Earth's surface. It often refers to the warming that occurs due to increased greenhouse gas emissions. *Climate change* (which is becoming the preferred term of use) refers to any significant change in measures of climate (e.g., temperature, precipitation, or wind) lasting for an extended period. Both events can be linked to natural and human activities. See www.epa.gov/climatechange/basicinfo.html to learn more.

capture what they know, to explore solutions to problems, to explain new constructs, or to redefine known ones. By investigating ideas, they refine their knowledge. It is this process that we are calling responsive writing, and we envision a re-crafting of text as writers talk and write with each other. Responsive writing gives students valuable opportunities to sort through the information gathered and to answer two important questions: "What do we have?" and "What can we do with it?" For example, students who engaged in the previous chapter's social studies lesson on the Industrial Age could gather in small groups to synthesize the information they found as they researched the topic. They could talk about what questions their information about the Industrial Age raises as we approach the Digital Age. They could use text, graphics, and other media to compose a representation of their group's understandings. With the help of technology, the sorting, editing, and reflecting become a much more collaborative endeavor than it would be in a traditional face-to-face classroom activity. That kind of computer-supported activity is responsive writing, and it will be explained within the context of a lesson plan. First, we will briefly describe the benefits of **collaborative learning**.

Collaborative Learning

Collaborative learning in a responsive writing frame is the lively interaction that occurs when minds are in the act of inquiry, of discovery, of making sense of a construct by attempting to define or label it. It is a process that involves questioning, challenging, and validating the ideas written by each member of the group.

A collaborative learning environment moves away from strategies that philosopher Paulo Freire (1970) likened to a bank transaction. That is, information is deposited by instructors into students like money is deposited into a bank. Why is it important for students to engage in this kind of learning? Freire would argue that collaborative learning requires research, critical thinking, resourcefulness, and an ability to conceptualize abstractly. Just like the team of NASA scientists who joined intellectual forces to bring back the Apollo 13 astronauts, today's digital natives working in response groups band together for a purpose. Another philosopher and educator, John Dewey, would likely applaud this form of having students collaborate to do the work of the real world because he believed that education is a social process. This kind of activity is an illustration of a popular Dewey quote: "We only think when we are confronted with a problem."

Collaborative and cooperative learning activities in today's diverse classrooms are particularly helpful for those students whose first language is not English. English language learners (ELLs) at the secondary level need opportunities to develop relationships with peers and to find support structures that will help them achieve success in an English-speaking learning environment. Studies show that group activities that are engaging and that tap into the knowledge that ELLs bring to the table will motivate all students to learn. The social process observed when students work in groups to solve a problem is the basis of a well-known strategy for helping students make sense of information: **Group Mapping Activity (GMA)** (Davidson, 1982). Students studying the scientific method in a science class, for instance, may use the Group Mapping Activity to collaboratively draft a hypothesis related to how the Black Sea was formed. Current theory holds that a great flood that occurred during the Ice Age filled a freshwater lake and the farmland around it, forming the Black Sea. After investigating a number of resources explaining the legend, theory, and scientific data related to the formation of the Black Sea, students engage in dialogue that leads to a collective understanding of the findings and a consensus on what a hypothesis might be for further study. This information can be represented in a conceptual map to show the logical support for the hypothesis.

> **Group Mapping Activity (GMA)**
> The Group Mapping Activity is a strategy designed to help students make sense of information. By using concept maps created on paper and/or online, students arrange information in ways that depict the meaning of terms and concepts and the connections between and among them.

The lesson described is an adaptation of a lesson entitled "The Scientific Method in Undersea Archaeology," which can be found at www.nationalgeographic. com. GMA and how it can be used with technology will be discussed more fully in the lesson plan that explores responsive writing.

How Does a Collaborative Environment Philosophy Fit in Responsive Writing?

In Chapter 2, we examined why making personal connections with the information being studied is important, and we discussed how a constructivist learning theory and philosophy supports teaching practices that make it possible for students to make personal connections. In this chapter we discuss the value of allowing students to work in groups to share what they know and to build new knowledge. How groups are arranged and guided through a learning activity can vary, so there are a number of labels for instructional practices: collaborative learning, cooperative learning, peer teaching, reciprocal learning, literacy circles or study circles, and work groups. In addition, some group activities are more formal than others (Johnson, Johnson, & Smith, 1991). That is, a group activity can be short and quick—to answer a question, for instance, or work through a math problem. Groups can have a more intensive purpose, though, like arriving at consensus about a moral issue or designing and producing a multimedia product. That kind of group activity would take more time and resources.

We will refer to group learning activities, regardless of the configuration or time students spend working together, as collaborative learning. Theorists and teachers have used this term for more than two decades to describe active student participation in an exchange of ideas that leads to more than simply completing a task. Collaborative learning, and in this case, collaborative *writing*, should be distinguished from another often-used label, cooperative learning. Panitz (1996) explains that collaborative learning is student focused while cooperative learning is teacher centered. He notes that the goal of the collaborative learning model is to arrive at a group consensus, to rely on creativity and innovation in order to make sense of and solve complex problems. In cooperative learning models, the goal is to collectively arrive at a predetermined right or wrong answer—not the kind of thinking that we are advocating in lessons that address **responsive writing**.

Collaborative learning in a responsive writing frame is the lively interaction that occurs when minds are in the act of inquiry, of discovery, of making sense of a construct by attempting to define or label it.

> **Responsive Writing**
> Students work in groups that communicate in person as easily as they do online through the use of blogs, wikis, and course management systems. They may also use online tools to collaboratively write with people beyond their school and community.

It is a process that involves questioning, challenging, and validating the ideas written by each member of the group. This kind of learning environment is strongly supported by research that shows that students who learn in small groups think at higher levels and retain information longer than students who work alone (Johnson & Johnson, 1986; Totten, Sills, Digby, & Russ, 1991).

A sister to the collaborative learning philosophy is inquiry models of teaching. Let's go back to Freire's bank transaction analogy in which the instructor deposits information in the students as one would deposit money in a bank. To extend the metaphor of knowledge as money, inquiry learning is more like playing the classic board game Monopoly. The teacher provides the game materials, explains the rules, and watches as the exchange of play money mimics transactions that occur in a real-world economy. Students must take chances, strategize, negotiate, and think in order to be economically successful in the game. In the same way, students must take chances, strategize, negotiate, and think to arrive at those "aha" moments when complex concepts become clear.

J. Richard Suchman, the originator of an inquiry teaching program that was widely used throughout the United States in the 1960s (see Suchman, 1968), once said that "inquiry is the way people learn when they're left alone." Dewey (1938/1997) would agree and argue that schools should provide a space for this kind of learning. He wrote, "There is an intimate and necessary relation between the processes of actual experience and education" (p. 20). Inquiry learning philosophy and its associated models like discovery learning are supported by a number of renowned theorists and psychologists such as Jean Piaget, Jerome Bruner, and Seymour Papert. Bruner (1967) refers to the "information drift," or the distraction that occurs when adolescents are learning information that may not be useful to them. He notes that discovery in learning leads learners to purposeful knowledge, information that can be used to solve actual problems.

Research on inquiry learning maintains that learning takes place most notably in problem-solving situations where the learner draws on his own experience and prior knowledge to discover truths about a subject. It is a personal, internal, and constructivist environment. In the study of writing, collaborative and discovery learning are most evident in the use of response groups. Leading proponents of teaching adolescents the process of writing have for decades advocated the use of collaborative groups. Peter Elbow (1973) talked about "teacherless writing groups"; Donald Murray (1982) suggested that teachers show students how to respond to writing; Lucy Calkins (1983) showed how using peer response groups brings positive benefits; Ken Macrorie (1984) discussed the value of "Helping Circles" in writing; James Moffett (1983) showed teachers how to help students teach each other; and Kenneth Bruffee (1983) stressed that writers need to talk through the task of writing. All wrote that collaborative learning in the writing workshop is essential.

Collaboration among writers in all subjects, not just English language arts, reduces writing anxiety and helps writers to overcome some of the difficulties they encounter in getting started. If they are preparing a document for a particular audience, they revise multiple times, each time contributing and responding until they achieve just the right length, tone, diction, and syntax for the purpose.

Responsive writing in a science class can transform a lesson so that it appeals to the digital native. Imagine Tomas, a seventh grader who is about to engage in learning about environmental systems. During the inside writing frame of this lesson, Tomas would have had opportunities to explore and investigate to find the information he needs to make personal connections with information about the earth's renewable, nonrenewable, and inexhaustible resources. As Tomas begins to think about responsive writing, he brings that information to a group of peers. He will share what he gathered in order to validate his knowledge. As a member of a formal learning group, he will question the information his peers have gathered as much as he will question his own.

What Is a Good Responsive Writing Lesson?

Tomas's science teacher assigns a project to synthesize what he and his classmates have gathered regarding ways in which natural events and human activity or a combination of both alter earth systems. In the process of their inside writing, Tomas and his classmates used the Web to investigate natural catastrophic events such as volcanic eruptions, hurricanes, and tsunamis as well as the effects of man-made disasters including large-scale oil spills, nuclear accidents, and the use of weapons of mass destruction. Through their investigations, they were able to make inferences and draw conclusions about the effects of human activity and natural catastrophes on renewable, nonrenewable, and inexhaustible resources. To prepare for the culmination of the unit, the teacher narrowed the focus and asked students to gather information from two specific time periods—global warming in the 21st century and the Dust Bowl of the 1930s. Now that the gathering is complete, the students are asked to synthesize their information using GMA.

The GMA lesson that follows would likely take place near the end of a unit of study that extends over two or more weeks. Prior to this lesson, students would have formed groups of four to engage in the inside writing practice described in Chapter 2. Two in each group would have gathered information on global warming while the other two would have focused on the Dust Bowl. This lesson would occur after information has been gathered, and although the lesson is designed to establish a setting for the collaborative learning that typifies what we call responsive writing, students would have engaged in collaborative activity within their groups before this lesson. The group presentations at the end of the GMA lesson could be the beginning of the culminating, or final, activity for the unit, or it could be a transitional closure of one day's lesson, which means that the results of the group work would be discussed in subsequent lessons in the unit. For instance, the comparisons made through GMA could be the basis of a multigenre group research project. Each member could write in one or more of a number of genres (see Table 3.1) to represent the information the group gathered and the knowledge that they constructed together. (For more information on multigenre writing, see Tom Romano's *Blending Genre, Altering Style*, 2000.)

Table 3.1   Writing Genres

Adventure	Fanfiction	Op-ed
Advertisement	Fantasy	Personal narrative
Biography	Historical fiction	Persuasive essay
Blog	Informational report	Poetry
Comedy	Interview	Political cartoon
Creative nonfiction	Journal	Pro/con
Drama	Letter	Review
Descriptive	Media article	Satire
Editorial	Multimedia presentation	Science fiction
Essay	Mystery	Speech
Fairy tale	Myth	Technical

Group Mapping Activity (GMA) Lesson Plan

Materials

- poster boards
- markers
- tape or thumbtacks for displaying posters
- sticky notes

Goal

Students understand how natural events and human activity can alter Earth systems.

Rationale

All life depends on environmental and climatic conditions. Because humans are the primary caretakers of the earth, students must learn about the effects of human activity on the environment. Students should understand how local and global natural and man-made events will impact their lives now and in the future.

Content Standard from the National Council of Teachers of Science

As a result of activities in grades 5–8, all students should develop understanding of personal health; populations, resources, and environments; natural hazards; risks and benefits; and science and technology in society.

- Internal and external processes of the Earth system cause natural hazards—events that change or destroy human or wildlife habitats, damage property, and harm or kill humans.

- Human activity also can induce hazards through resource acquisition, urban growth, land-use decisions, and waste disposal. Such activities can accelerate many natural changes.

Objectives

- Students will illustrate similarities and differences between global warming and the Dust Bowl using facts arranged in a graphic organizer.
- Students will explain their graphic organizers to the class.

Group Mapping Activity (GMA) Lesson Plan (cont'd)

Activities

- Introduction: On an index card, ask students to quickly write one fact about global warming or the Dust Bowl that they found most fascinating without stating "global warming" or "Dust Bowl." Collect cards and randomly select five to eight cards to read. As each card is read, ask students to guess to which concept the fact is referring. Tell students that they will be comparing and contrasting facts about these two topics.

- Activity 1: Demonstrate various forms of graphic organizers and ask groups to suggest ideas for other forms of graphic organizers.

- Activity 2: Ask groups to create a graphic organizer that shows the similarities and differences between the Dust Bowl and global warming. Give them poster boards and markers for this activity.

- Activity 3: Ask each group to present the poster and display it on a wall or bulletin board for all to see.

- Closure: Allow time for a "gallery walk"—students walk around the room to view posters and write comments on sticky notes that are adhered to the posters.

Modifications

Working in groups and organizing information in conceptual maps are ways to address the diverse needs of students. Providing a means for them to express their knowledge orally, in writing, and in a poster demonstration gives all learners, and English language learners (ELLs) in particular, opportunities to practice various language skills. Providing magazines and other materials with photos that can be cut out and added to posters will help ELLs use images to enhance their expression of their new knowledge.

Assessment

Formative assessment—teacher evaluation of quality of facts and effectiveness of organization of ideas on conceptual maps through observation and questioning.

How Is a Good Responsive Writing Lesson Made Better?

Students share, question, edit, and reflect on information during this GMA lesson—clearly they are benefiting from learning in a collaborative environment. Tomas's teacher acts as a catalyst, someone who inspires and nudges the groups in her class to come to a consensus and produce a poster that shows logical thinking. However, even before that finished poster is thumb-tacked to the wall, the collaborative dialog may fade. Multitasking digital natives might be more motivated to create online conceptual maps that are rich, multidimensional representations of their thinking and that are pinned to a *virtual* wall and can be modified at any time. That is, the concept maps could include links to websites, movie clips, audio clips, and so forth, and could be viewed, added to, or commented on online by their team and others. (See www.shambles.net/pages/school/mindmaps for a comprehensive list of downloadable and online concept-mapping programs.)

As discussed in Chapter 1, digital natives are as comfortable using Facebook as they are talking face-to-face. The teacher who is aware of digital natives' ways of composing and communicating may shift from the role of a catalyst to that of a curator in a technology-supported lesson. As a catalyst, the teacher manages group behavior in the manner described in this GMA lesson. As a curator, the teacher has charge of a collection of student knowledge much like a museum curator has charge of a diverse collection of priceless items. Her goal is to design a method for organizing and showcasing the collection of student knowledge so that it validates different perspectives. In this role, she can provide the online organizing tools to display evolving conceptual maps, and she can create an online forum to encourage ongoing dialogue. The maps and the forum could be opened to other classes, schools, communities, or the Web population at large. The GMA lesson, then, could provide more visibility of ideas, more sharing, and more awareness of varying perspectives both among classmates and among users of online collaborative spaces in general.

Wiki
Like blogs, wikis are online spaces for writing and posting. A wiki allows writers to work on one document that is stored online and can be accessed through the Internet. Wikis also allow students to store pictures, graphics, movies, and other objects.

Digital natives who use **wikis** (like Wikipedia) have learned that information is in a constant state of change and that they play a collaborative part in that motion because they have the freedom and power to add to, sort through, and redefine information. For Tomas, questioning and challenging the information his peers and others post on a teacher-created wiki enables him to offer his unique perspective and validate his new knowledge. This kind of collaborative learning is what we call responsive writing.

Collaborating in a Digital Way

Tomas will often surf along the Web, but sometimes he will troll, dragging his net slowly along the depths of the Web to find treasures. He may pull up information and ask, "Is it valuable or not?" When he decides it is valuable, he can post his interpretation of it in the group/class blog or wiki. Tomas may want to express himself with text as well as with images, sounds, and video he finds. Even if he feels his information or ideas are valid, once they are posted, they become part of a collective knowledge and may be modified

as they undergo co-construction. Tomas's ideas may be challenged by group members who, in a collaborative spirit, will determine what is valuable to all members of the group. Of all the tools available on Web 2.0 for this kind of dialogue, blogs and wikis are the easiest to use. Websites like Blogger and Wordpress allow teachers and students to establish a group exchange. Wikispaces and pbwiki, too, are user-friendly spaces for collaborative writing. According to Will Richardson (2006), a noted advocate of using online communication in schools, when students use tools like these, ". . . they are not only learning how to publish content; they are also learning how to develop and use all sorts of collaborative skills, negotiating with others to agree on correctness, meaning, relevance, and more" (p. 65). Tomas may think he's working with a group in a fun way and not know that he is in fact learning the collaborative skills that are critical in today's global, digital society. In the case of this GMA lesson plan, the Web 2.0 tools that can be used for responsive writing are vehicles for deciding what it means to be a responsible human in charge of a seemingly fragile earth.

What Is a Good Digital Version of a Responsive Writing Lesson?

The following lesson is a remake of the previous GMA lesson. It still uses GMA as the strategy and has an identical goal, rationale, objectives, and lesson introduction. The procedures and materials reflect online collaboration using an Internet classroom assistant (ICA)[2] such as www.nicenet.org or www.moodle.org.

---

[2]An *Internet classroom assistant* (ICA) is an online communication and classroom management tool that provides Web-based messaging and conferencing between a teacher and students. It also allows designated members to post and share documents, links, messages, and schedules so that all members have access to classroom conversations, information, and resources.

GMA Lesson Plan—The ReMake

Materials

- computers and projector
- Internet access
- Internet classroom assistant (such as www.nicenet.org)
- concept-mapping software or freeware (Inspiration, FreeMind, etc.)
- class wiki

Goal

Students understand how natural events and human activity can alter Earth systems.

Rationale

All life depends on environmental and climatic conditions. Because humans are the primary caretakers of the Earth, students must learn about the effects of human activity on the environment. Students should understand how local and global natural and man-made events will impact their lives now and in the future.

Content Standard from the National Council of Teachers of Science

As a result of activities in grades 5–8, all students should develop understanding of personal health; populations, resources, and environments; natural hazards; risks and benefits; and science and technology in society.

- Internal and external processes of the Earth system cause natural hazards—events that change or destroy human or wildlife habitats, damage property, and harm or kill humans.

- Human activity also can induce hazards through resource acquisition, urban growth, land-use decisions, and waste disposal. Such activities can accelerate many natural changes.

GMA Lesson Plan—The ReMake (cont'd)

Objectives

- Students will illustrate similarities and differences between global warming and the Dust Bowl using facts arranged in a digital graphic organizer.

- Students will explain their graphic organizers to the class and then post them to a class wiki.

Activities

- Introduction: On an index card, ask students to quickly write one fact about global warming or the Dust Bowl that they found most fascinating without stating "global warming" or "Dust Bowl." Collect cards and randomly select between five and eight cards to read. As each card is read, ask students to guess to which concept the fact is referring. Tell students that they will be comparing and contrasting facts about these two topics.

- Activity 1: Establish a course using an Internet classroom assistant like www.nicenet.org or www.moodle.org and group students in sets of four: two who investigated the Dust Bowl and two who investigated global warming. Ask students to use the discussion board to share their findings.

- Activity 2: After discussing their findings, ask groups to use Inspiration or some other concept-mapping program to draft a graphic design that shows the similarities and differences between the Dust Bowl and global warming. Encourage them to include Web links, photos, etc., on their maps. Allow students at least forty-five minutes to create the conceptual maps.

- Activity 3: Ask each group to present their map to the class (using a projector) and then post their map to a class wiki. (Maps can be saved as images and uploaded into the wiki.)

- Closure: Allow time for groups to go online to view each map and to post comments, add information, etc.

GMA Lesson Plan—The ReMake (cont'd)

Modifications

As in the original plan, working in groups, organizing information in conceptual maps, and creating a means for expressing knowledge creatively are ways to address the diverse needs of students in this makeover. However, in addition to these supports, technology makes available a seemingly boundless bank of photos, movies, sounds, and graphics. English language learners will have multiple opportunities to engage in reading, writing, and talking and will have access to information that is visual, auditory, and presented in various languages.

Assessment

Formative assessment—teacher evaluation of quality of facts and effectiveness of organization of ideas on conceptual maps through observation and questioning.

The responsive writing experience described in this GMA lesson may build confidence in adolescents by putting them in an environment where they learn how to write collaboratively, how to use Netiquette specific to wikis, and how to negotiate language so that it is clear and purposeful. An awareness of self and group might prompt Tomas to want to connect with a larger response group, one that can be found in blogs and wikis that are created by and for people who want to engage in global conversations and the co-construction of knowledge.

Tomas may even be inspired to return to the inside writing he had engaged in earlier in the lesson and find more information online about either the Dust Bowl or global warming or both. For instance, he could watch excerpts from *The Plow That Broke the Plains* (Lorentz, 1936), a government-sponsored, twenty-five-minute video produced in the 1930s (found at www.archive.org, a nonprofit Internet library), and excerpts from *An Inconvenient Truth* (Guggenheim, 2006), former Vice President Al Gore's movie, filmed seven decades later, about global warming and its impact on the environment. Tomas could listen to audio files of songs written during the Dust Bowl era or view Melissa Etheridge's (2006) music video about global warming, *I Need to Wake Up*, on YouTube. He could read journal entries from survivors of the Dust Bowl and excerpts from Timothy Egan's award-winning *The Worst Hard Time: The Untold Story of Those Who Survived the Great American Dust Bowl* (2006). To learn more about global warming, he could visit websites such as www.NOAA.gov (the National Oceanic and Atmospheric Association) to read about the Global Earth Observation System, a U.S.-led initiative of more than sixty countries with an aim to "make 21st century technology as interrelated as the planet it observes, predicts and protects, providing the science on which sound policy and decision-making must be built." He could also visit YouTube to watch video clips of dust storms from 1930s Oklahoma or the present-day Middle East. Or Tomas could watch any of the more than 20,000 short videos there that are related to one of the urgent international concerns of his future, global warming. Most important, as a young consumer of information, he could critically assess the credibility and value of the sources he has located.

As his knowledge of science, the environment, and society grows, he may feel confident enough to contribute to Wikipedia's explanation of these concepts, and of the Dust Bowl and global warming, in particular. Or he may explore wikis such as http://globalwarming.wikidot.com/ or www.wikihow.com/Main-Page. Both sites are visited by people who have information to share about global warming. Ideally, Tomas may decide to create his own wiki and invite others to write with him. How Tomas's teacher helps him do this, how she helps him transition from a local writer to a global writer, becomes more important than ever. In the classroom, she has been working in the role of curator, guiding students' contributions to the class wiki by ensuring that what a student posts is of value to the response group and to the whole group. As she guides Tomas in his attempt to do the same thing in a much larger virtual space such as Wikipedia, she collaborates with him to decide how his contribution adds value to the collection of information that is already there. She might ask him questions such as "What have you read on this wiki? What do you think you would like to add? Why is that a good thing to add?" She may also decide to establish a collaborative wiki relationship between Tomas and his class and another group of students on the other side of the globe. The Flat Classroom Project, an award-winning educational wiki, is a noteworthy example of a collaborative study of Thomas Friedman's *The World Is Flat* (2005), a popular book about the rapidly changing global economy. In this project, students in Georgia and Bangladesh used a wiki to co-construct their context-specific interpretations of Friedman's provocative ideas about globalization in the 21st century. In a recent project initiated within the wiki—the Digiteen Global Project—classrooms from across the globe came together to engage in discussions about digital citizenship, specifically, how to behave appropriately and responsibly when using technology.

From group dialogue to one-on-one collaboration with the teacher, ideas created by digital natives like Tomas can be launched to a global collaborative writing forum. Responsive writing takes on a new dimension, one that could only be possible in a technology-rich classroom.

How Do We Know That Tomas Is Learning?

At this point, you might ask, "Isn't the GMA just as valuable a learning experience with a poster board and markers as it is with a wiki?" You may worry that a group activity that occurs in a classroom as well as online may stray from the lesson plan and particularly from a manageable design for assessment. There is a natural desire to establish what is right or wrong and to measure student outcomes using a common yardstick. Certainly you can facilitate a very effective lesson with posters and markers, and assigning a grade to a poster hanging on the wall can motivate students. But ask a group of digital natives where they would like their work to appear, and the majority will answer, "On the Web!"

How does a teacher evaluate something less tangible than a poster on a wall? It's a challenging question, and as more teachers make the leap to a digital classroom, they will need to find alternative forms of assessment. Marzano, Pickering, and McTighe (1993) outline a standards-based method for evaluating student work. The quality of content knowledge (what information students know) and procedural knowledge (what skills students have) is based on rubrics created *by and for students*. It is worthwhile to note that students and the teacher can collaborate to construct rubrics on a class wiki. Granted, evaluating student performance in a digital environment can be messy business, but being a curator among a highly motivated group of contributors can be exciting for the teacher and her students, as our observations of digital natives Daniel and Nicole showed.

Daniel and Nicole's response to the Dust Bowl/global warming assignment described in this chapter indicated that we are on the right digital track. As the teacher explained the GMA, Daniel and Nicole acted like typical seventh graders. Their reaction was a mixture of deep sighs and compliance followed by, "How long does this have to be?" and "Is this for a grade?" When they learned that their work would be posted to a wiki, however, their attitudes transformed from resigned students to motivated learners.

During inside writing, Daniel and Nicole shared, sorted, and questioned information about the Dust Bowl and global warming. Daniel had never heard of the Dust Bowl, but he was undaunted. Quick searches on Google and Wikipedia led him to a wealth of information. He was intrigued by the archived photos and films, and he was anxious to share the new information with Nicole. As with so many digital natives, their conversation began in front of computers, and Daniel would frequently say to the Nicole, "Look at this." Nicole would instantly lean over to absorb information Daniel had uncovered. Nicole, the designated global-warming expert, also found a wealth of information, but because her topic deals primarily with future projections, she did not find the powerful, emotion-filled images Daniel discovered. Instead, she found maps and charts and an occasional satirical cartoon commenting on the political tension around global warming. Nicole was not able to connect to the learning as quickly as Daniel, but she began to drill, a skill we referred to in the previous chapter. Nicole remembered a connection between global warming and the polar bears' natural habitat. She refined her search, and within minutes she was gathering information about the polar ice caps, endangered species, and predictions about future global temperatures. She, too, began to say, "Look at this," and Daniel took time out from his search to examine the new information. As Daniel and Nicole leaned from one screen to another, they read information, pointed to images, asked questions, commented on interesting and alarming facts, and sought validation from each other. Two heads moved from one screen to another in a clearly collaborative style.

Because the inside writing stage became a collaborative activity, Daniel and Nicole moved seamlessly from inside to responsive writing. In fact, the basic framework for their graphic organizer had been constructed as they shared information during the initial search. Through their conversations, Daniel and Nicole identified differences and similarities between the Dust Bowl and global warming. They also came to the realization that natural events and human activity—past, present, and future—have a profound impact on the environment and on the wellbeing of earth's occupants, a very personal and powerful connection for two seventh graders to make.

Daniel and Nicole were able to quickly and easily create a graphic organizer to display their new learning, but they did not rely solely on text. They imported images to illustrate their information and to make the emotional connections they had experienced moments earlier. They also added links to favorite sites that contained video and audio files. The digital natives are not content to work only with text. For them, images, sound, and movement add meaning to words. The images of a tenant farmer digging out from an inland dune or a video of a displaced polar bear in search of food will fuel impassioned discussion, face-to-face and online.

After presenting their conceptual maps, Daniel and Nicole and their classmates saved their maps as image files and uploaded them into the class wiki. Just as their teacher planned, a collaborative activity between small groups of students grew into a whole-group project. The information posted on the wiki is now available to all of her students, and she guides them as they add to, edit, question, and redraft in a continuous process that will strengthen their understandings and connections to a very timely topic. As Nicole sees it, posting class work to the Web is an added technological bonus. "If I'm at home, and I think about a change I want to make to our wiki, I can do it right then. The teacher might not give me time in the classroom, or it might be a week before we get to go back to the computer lab."

For digital natives, posting work to a wiki is deemed far more valuable, more important than completing traditional pen and paper work. According to Daniel, "I can upload more things like pictures and videos. I have more freedom when I work on the Web."

Chapter Summary

If we did a GMA comparing the philosophies of Freire and Dewey with the 21st century projections in Friedman's book, one overarching notion would emerge: adolescents must know how to collaborate and solve real-world problems. Responsive writing, which follows inside writing, meets that need for learning collaborative skills and can be enhanced using strategies, like GMA, that are based in real-world settings. Web 2.0 tools and the social networking systems that they support are designed for such collaboration. Digital natives are accustomed to using Facebook and Wikipedia, for instance, but these young writers may not have the social skills to respond appropriately and the language skills to communicate with clarity. In a time when teachers feel that they are competing with game systems, iPods, and cell phones, it is comforting to realize that you still play an important role in an adolescent's education. Teachers who use responsive writing strategies engage adolescents in face-to-face and online dialogue, and their students learn to thoughtfully negotiate the language of Web 2.0—text, images, sound, and video—as they write. By becoming competent and confident communicators, they are ready to move into the next frame—purposeful writing. They are ready to write with a particular audience in mind.

Responsive Writing Practice in Social Studies, Math, and English Language Arts

To practice ways of remaking a lesson plan so that it addresses responsive writing, use the sample science remake lesson as a guide to designing a plan that uses GMA in social studies, math, or English language arts.

Social Studies: In a social studies class, focus on government response to natural disasters. You could take a historical approach by investigating government-sponsored relief during the Dust Bowl era, the Mount Saint Helen's eruption, the Galveston Hurricane, or the Molasses Disaster of 1919. For a more current study, investigate government response following Hurricane Katrina or look at current efforts to deal with global warming. Ask students to work within groups, each group producing a letter written from the perspective of a disaster survivor. Remind group members to share information gathered during inside writing and to reach a consensus when writing their letter. Each group can use a page in the class wiki to collaboratively compose its letter.

Address this curriculum standard from the National Council for the Social Studies—Thematic Strand III: People, Places, and Environments:

- Social studies programs should include experiences that provide for the study of people, places, and environments so that the learner can:
  - observe and speculate about social and economic effects of environmental changes and crises resulting from phenomena such as floods, storms, and drought.

Math: Ask students to gather data about average temperatures, precipitation rates, population growth, and water consumption in your area over the last twenty years. Using that data, identify patterns and make predictions about future trends. Working in groups, students can create a chart or graph (using InspireData or Excel) to illustrate historical data and their projections. On the class wiki, each group can post its graphic representation and explain how they used past data to make future predictions. You can also launch a joint investigation with another classroom in another region to compare information.

Address this content standard from the National Council of Teachers of Mathematics (grades 6–8):

- Work flexibly with fractions, decimals, and percents to solve problems.

English Language Arts: Begin a study of an author's use of words by reading a book based on the Dust Bowl experience. For lower grades, you might use Karen Hesse's *Out of the Dust* (1997). For upper grades, you could use John Steinbeck's *The Grapes of Wrath* (1967) or Timothy Egan's *The Worst Hard Time* (2006). During reading, ask students to collect powerful words, phrases, and images from the reading and deposit them in a class wiki. As a culminating activity, divide students into groups and ask them to write a found poem about global warming using the words, phrases, and images collected during reading. To prepare students for the found poem activity, lead them to websites such as http://green.nationalgeographic.com/environment.

Address this content standard from the National Council of Teachers of English:

- Students develop an understanding of and respect for diversity in language use, patterns, and dialects across cultures, ethnic groups, geographic regions, and social roles.

Table 3.2 Resources for Responsive Writing

Responsive Writing Processes	Web Links and Tools Used in Science ReMake Lesson
Labeling	Inspiration FreeMind MS Word software/freeware for mind mapping MS Word software for word processing
Questioning and Challenging	www.blogger.com www.wordpress.com online interactive journals (blogs) www.nicenet.org Internet classroom assistant (ICA)
Validating	www.wikispaces.com www.pbwiki.com online collaborative writing spaces

Discussion Questions

1. How can the remake lesson described in this chapter be modified to fit in your classroom and to meet the needs of your students? If you are not teaching yet, consider how the remake lesson could be modified to fit a classroom you have observed.

2. While completing a technology-based GMA activity, what are online access options available to you for gathering information, posting student work, and facilitating ongoing edits, revisions, and additions from students?

3. What is an effective lesson that can be made better by using the GMA strategy and technology?

References

Bruffee, K. A. (1983). Writing and reading as collaborative or social acts. In J. N. Hays, P. A. Roth, J. R. Ramsey, & R. D. Foulke (Eds.), *The writer's mind: Writing as a mode of thinking*, pp. 159–169. Urbana, IL: NCTE.

Bruner, J. S. (1967). *On knowing: Essays for the left hand*. Cambridge, MA: Harvard University Press.

Calkins, L. M. (1983). *Lessons from a child: On the teaching and learning of writing*. Portsmouth, NH: Heinemann.

Cecez-Kecmanovic, D., & Webb, C. (2000). A critical inquiry into Web-mediated collaborative learning. In A. Aggarwal (Ed.), *Web-based learning and teaching technologies: Opportunities and challenges* (pp. 307–326). Hershey, PA: Idea Group.

Davidson, J. L. (1982). The group mapping activity for instruction in reading and thinking. *Journal of Reading, 26*, 52–56.

Dewey, J. (1938/1997). *Experience and education*. New York: Macmillan.

Egan, T. (2006). *The worst hard time: The untold story of those who survived the great American Dust Bowl*. New York: Mariner Books.

Elbow, P. (1973). *Writing without teachers*. New York: Oxford.

Etheridge, M. (2006). *I need to wake up* [Music video]. USA: Universal Music Group. Retrieved March 29, 2009, from www.youtube.com/watch?v=djP-c7d_Oeo.

Freire, P. (1970). *Pedagogy of the oppressed.* New York: Herder and Herder.

Friedman, T. (2005). *The world is flat.* New York: Farrar, Straus and Giroux.

Graves, D. (1983). *Writing: Teachers and children at work.* Portsmouth, NH: Heinemann.

Graves, D. (1984). *A researcher learns to write: Selected articles and monographs.* Portsmouth, NH: Heinemann.

Grazer, B. (Producer), & Howard, R. (Director). (1995). *Apollo 13* [Motion picture]. USA: Universal Pictures.

Guggenheim, D. (Director). (2006). *An inconvenient truth* [Motion picture]. USA: Paramount Pictures.

Hesse, K. (1997). *Out of the dust.* New York: Scholastic.

Johnson, D. W., Johnson, R. T., & Smith, K. A. (1991). *Cooperative learning: Increasing college faculty instructional productivity.* ASHE-FRIC Higher Education Report No. 4. Washington, DC: School of Education and Human Development, George Washington University.

Johnson, R. T., & Johnson, D. W. (1986). Action research: Cooperative learning in the science classroom. *Science and Children, 24,* 31–32.

Lorentz, P. (Director). (1936). *The plow that broke the plains* [Motion picture]. United States: U.S. Resettlement Administration.

Macrorie, K. (1984). *Writing to be read.* Upper Montclair, NJ: Boynton/Cook.

Marzano, R. J., Pickering, D., & McTighe, J. (1993). *Assessing student outcomes: Performance assessment using the Dimensions of Learning Model.* Alexandria, VA: ASCD.

Moffett, J. (1983). *Teaching the universe of discourse.* Boston: Houghton Mifflin.

Murray, D. (1982). *Learning by teaching: Selected articles on writing and teaching.* Upper Montclair, NJ: Boynton/Cook.

Panitz, T. (1996). Collaborative versus cooperative learning—A comparison of the two concepts which will help us understand the underlying nature of interactive learning. Retrieved May 14, 2008, from http://pirun.ku.ac.th/~btun/pdf/coop_collab.pdf.

Richardson, W. (2006). *Blogs, wikis, podcasts, and other powerful web tools for classrooms.* Thousand Oaks, CA: Corwin Press.

Romano, T. (2000). *Blending genre, altering style*. Portsmouth, NH: Heinemann.

Steinbeck, J. (1967). *The grapes of wrath*. New York: Penguin Books.

Suchman, J. R. (1968). *Developing inquiry in earth science*. Chicago, IL: Science Research Associates.

Totten, S., Sills, T., Digby, A., & Russ, P. (1991). *Cooperative learning: A guide to research*. New York: Garland.

Ventimiglia, Laura M. (1993). Cooperative learning at the college level. *NEA Higher Education Journal*, 5–30.

Purposeful Writing

Key Elements in Chapter 4

Purposeful Writing In this frame, writers use Web 2.0 tools to investigate a topic as well as to present their interpretation of the topic for others on the Web to review. The goal is to create and deliver information with a particular audience in mind.

Information Processing Theory This theory explains how we store information in short-term and long-term memory and how we access that information when it is needed. Self-monitoring—being aware of inputting new information—is critical in the learning process.

Vocabulary Self-Collection Strategy (VSS) Vocabulary Self-Collection Strategy is a strategy for learning new terms and concepts. By selecting words while investigating information and creating a personal glossary, students can take an active role in learning, or can self-monitor learning.

Cyber Word Wall A cyber word wall is like a physical word wall in the classroom, but it is online. It is a collection of terms and their meanings that can be created in a wiki or blog and that can be accessed by the creator, by people given access to it by the creator, or by anyone on the Web.

I want to get everything right because I want people to know exactly what I think.

Jordan, grade 10

Chapter Preview

The third frame of the writing experience is *purposeful writing*. Purposeful writing entails the use of precise language to explain something. Students who write purposefully arrange words so that the reader can easily make sense of what is written. For instance, a skillful writer drafting a biography carefully organizes facts about the person being investigated. When writing about a scientific experiment, a purposeful writer explains how she arrived at her conclusion by describing procedures in well-formed sentences that flow in logical progression. Technology enhances purposeful writing by adding dimension to this form of communication. For instance, creating a digital story about a person or constructing a website describing a science experiment enhances the message because visual images and auditory support can refine and/or elaborate ideas captured in words. As in the preceding chapters, this chapter will explore theoretical models for teaching and learning, namely, information processing theory. We will describe the makeover of a math lesson that uses a vocabulary-building strategy to help students communicate with precise language.

What Is Purposeful Writing?

Homer Hickam's autobiography, *The Rocket Boys* (1998), inspired *October Sky* (Gordon et al., 1999), a film about four high school friends growing up in a small coal-mining town in West Virginia. After the launch of Sputnik in 1957, the four set out to build and launch a model rocket. Building a rocket today is a relatively common hobby, but in America's post-McCarthyist 1950s, this kind of endeavor was viewed with suspicion. One person, however, openly supported the boys—their science teacher, Ms. Riley. She located a book entitled *Principles of Guided Missile Design* and encouraged them to use it as a guide for designing an experiment to showcase at the local science fair. They did, won first place, and continued to national competition where, against a number of odds, they won first place again. The science fair required the boys to write about their mathematical calculations in the kind of precise language that was used by the scientists who authored the book Ms. Riley located.

For Homer and his friends, writing was the only way their novel ideas could have been explained to the scientific community and justified to skeptics in their unsupportive town. Passion for rocketry was not enough to garner the first-place prize at the national science fair and the respect of family and friends. That happened because of the guidance and support they received from a teacher who introduced them to the logical organization and precise vocabulary used in scientific writing. It is the Rocket Boys' attention to this logical and precise writing that we are calling purposeful writing.

Purposeful writing is as critical in science class today as it was in Homer's 1950s, but precise and logical language is probably most critical in math class because numbers are the essence of digital information. A myriad of forms of math are used in daily life—math to figure out game scores, to explain financial trends, or to understand how an electoral vote differs from a popular vote in a presidential election. More than ever, our populace is working with gadgets and machines that translate our thoughts into animation, graphics, video, sound, and more by coding and arranging numbers. And it's interesting to note that the quintessential binary code (combinations of "1" and "0") makes up the language used by computer programmers and electrical engineers.

Among progressive math educators, the notion of *numeracy* or *quantitative literacy*—the ability to read, interpret, and/or apply numerical information—is as important as working with words. Numeracy has been compared to writing, and some propose that it be taught across the curriculum, too (Steen, 2001). Comprehending and communicating quantitative knowledge through words is key to being proficient in both numeracy and writing. As Mike Fletcher, a high school math teacher in Alabama, put it, ". . . if students read about concepts and learn the meanings of the words used to communicate mathematics . . . they will retain information longer and they will be able to relate different aspects of math that they had previously seen as irrelevant or disjointed" (Fletcher, 2003, p. 4). The National Council of Teachers of Math's Principles and Standards for School Mathematics states the following: "Students who have opportunities, encouragement, and support for speaking, writing, reading, and listening in mathematics classes reap dual benefits: they communicate to learn mathematics, and they learn to communicate mathematically" (NTCM, 2000). Yet writing is not often present in our schools' math classes. In their study of the National Assessment of Educational Progress (NAEP) report, Applebee and Langer (2006) noted that in 2002 only 13 percent of students wrote in math classes in the eighth grade. An even smaller percentage—approximately 8 percent—of twelfth graders reported being asked to complete a weekly writing assignment in their math class.

To understand what knowing math vocabulary means in the classroom, it is important to understand what happens in the brain. One view, **information processing theory**, explains learning in terms of mechanisms in the brain that control how we remember information and apply it in different settings. Information stored in memory is monitored by learners in a process called *self-modification*. Through self-modification, the learner uses knowledge and strategies acquired from earlier problem solving to modify a response to a new situation or problem. For instance, understanding the term *average* after learning how to calculate an average is necessary when a student is asked to find a mean for a set of data.

> **Information Processing Theory**
> This theory explains how we store information in short-term and long-term memory and how we access that information when it is needed. Self-monitoring—being aware of inputting new information—is critical in the learning process.

How might self-modification be taught? One way is to teach vocabulary—the labels for concepts, patterns, functions, and formulas. The **Vocabulary Self-Collection Strategy (VSS)** (Rapp, 1986) is a widely used method for guiding students through the creation of a word list that is meaningful to them. Vocabulary Self-Collection Strategy and math language can intersect favorably in a technology-supported classroom. Linking words to visual or auditory representations can reinforce existing knowledge and help construct new knowledge. How this happens will be discussed in a lesson plan that explores measures of central tendency (mean, median, mode).

> **Vocabulary Self-Collection Strategy (VSS)**
> Vocabulary Self-Collection Strategy is a strategy for learning new terms and concepts. By selecting words while investigating information and creating a personal glossary, students can take an active role in learning, or can self-monitor learning.

How Does Information Processing Fit in Purposeful Writing?

In Chapter 2, we discuss how inside writing is viewed through a constructivist learning theory lens—students make sense of information found online by relating it to their lives as they are constructing knowledge. Chapter 3 focuses on responsive writing, the kind of writing that is generated when writers work within an online collaborative learning environment. That is, they share their ideas, review each other's drafts, or coauthor a draft. What they generate, whether it is for a paper, a poster, a blog, a wiki, or a podcast, is the synthesis of gathered information and/or the creation of a new perspective. In the frame described in this chapter, **purposeful writing**, the ability to craft their ideas with accuracy and precision will be viewed from the perspective of theories that describe how thinking skills are developed: schema theory and information processing theory. Before we explain how these theories support our view of computer-supported writing within the purposeful writing frame, we will first discuss the importance of words. Knowing the vocabulary of a discipline like science or math can improve comprehension of that content's concepts. And vocabulary can ultimately be a gateway for entry into conversations that distinguish groups of like-minded people. Consequently, knowing the right words and how to use them is key to writing with a purpose and for a specific audience.

Purposeful Writing

In this frame, writers use Web 2.0 tools to investigate a topic as well as to present their interpretation of the topic for others on the Web to review. The goal is to create and deliver information with a particular audience in mind.

Decades of research on how we read support the following claims about the value of building vocabulary:

- The more words one knows, the better is the ability to comprehend text.

- The readability of text is determined by the difficulty of the words in the text.

- Families of words (example: spray, mist, steam, vapor) must be understood in the sense of how each word in a family is used.

- Simplifying vocabulary in text does not necessarily make text easier to comprehend.

Knowing words and the concepts they label has always been a staple of American curriculum, but how vocabulary has been taught has varied considerably. In many cases, learning new vocabulary means memorizing lists of words and definitions. More recently, however, that approach has given way to learning through application. Almost a century ago, John Dewey proposed that schools teach the skills required to succeed in life by emulating real-world activities in classroom activities. The reform-based emphasis on authentic instruction introduced in the early 1990s echoed Dewey's call for making school learning meaningful by connecting classroom learning to what happens in life. (See Newmann, 1993, for a succinct history of authentic instruction.) By purposefully mimicking the work of professionals, students develop the cognitive skills necessary to succeed in the real world. "Mimicking the work of professionals" means knowing the language of what can be labeled a "discourse community"—a group of people who share interests, values, or knowledge. For instance, dialogue among physicians will be quite different from dialogue among architects just as dialogue among teachers is different from business managers' conversations. Each professional group has its own vocabulary. Read a few pages in any magazine or journal about food, golf, art, psychology, or pop culture and you will learn the vocabulary, or lexicon, of that discourse community. A person's knowledge of the vocabulary of a discourse community often determines whether that person will be able to communicate with, and therefore align with, like-minded members of that group. That is, she will or will not be viewed as a member of that discourse community.

Purposeful writing relies intentionally on vocabulary—using the words that most precisely align with the lexicon of a discourse community. Psychologists have offered a number of theories to explain how we learn new words and how they become a part of our knowledge base. In the world of literacy research, we often refer to "schema theory" (Piaget, 1926), which explains how we make connections between what we know and what is unfamiliar in order to develop a knowledge base. Piaget used the term *assimilation* to describe the process of rearranging or revising what we know when we learn something new. It is the "aha" moment, when the once-unfamiliar idea, term, or concept suddenly makes sense. It makes sense because it has successfully connected with something we already know.

According to another theory, information processing theory, our short-term memory and long-term memory are activated when we process and store new information. Think of stored vocabulary as a pantry of ingredients needed to put together a wide array of recipes. A search on Wikipedia provided this description of information processing theory: "The human mind is a system that processes information through the application of logical rules and strategies" (Wikipedia, 2008). Certainly we do not always rely on Wikipedia, but in this case, the information is accurate. That is, it concurs with the psychology textbooks that define the theory and describe thinking as information processing that involves memory. According to these textbooks, there are four mechanisms that work together to bring about change in cognitive skills: encoding, strategy construction, automatization, and generalization. When information is encoded, it enters into the sensory register, then the short-term memory, and ultimately, the long-term memory, where it may be stored permanently and from which it may be later retrieved. A key precept in this theoretical model is self-modification. According to information processing theory, learners play an active role in their own development by transferring learned information and strategies to new situations or problems.

As stated earlier, students should be carefully examining the writing they generate to determine its purpose. Why use a particular format? Who is going to read it or view it? In other words, who is the audience or the intended discourse community? Is the vocabulary used appropriate? To illustrate how students can build vocabulary and use that knowledge for purposeful writing, we will describe Scott, a fictional eighth-grade math student. He and his peers are studying the concepts of *mean*, *median*, and *mode* in order to find the central tendency in collected data. They must analyze findings and write a report for the school board to review.

What Is a Good Purposeful Writing Lesson?

To deliver a clearly constructed message, a student must choose just the right vocabulary, images, and even sounds. The writer must then organize information so that it flows well, and revise and edit until what is being delivered is as clear as it can possibly be.

Scott's math teacher provides an opportunity for his class to gather and analyze data about how technology is used by teens. The students will write a summary of their study to present to the school board. To help the students with this writing project, Scott's teacher shows them how to use the VSS strategy to learn the vocabulary that mathematicians, pollsters, and policymakers use.

The VSS lesson that follows focuses on one or two days within a unit plan on measures of central tendency. To make the learning meaningful, Scott's teacher has asked the class to emulate a national study. Students will write a summary that is similar to the national sample. The teacher shows an excerpt from a technical report (Research Images, LLC, & Pew Internet and American Life Project, 2007):

> Some of our focus group participants reported using computers online from 12 to 20 hours per week, cell phones roughly 7 to 10 hours per week, and MP3 players or iPods about 2 to 4 hours per week. Boys reported that they spend about 2 to 4 hours per week playing computer and/or video games as well (younger boys report playing more). Teens did not report television or radio use on the surveys. However, we found that many watch

about 2 to 4 hours of television per week—or, as some reported, a personalized, on-demand media product such as a DVD, YouTube video, or the like. Thus, our teens seem to be spending from 25 to 42 hours per week using various technologies. Per day, that is 4 to 6 hours on average. Many teens noted that they multitask (i.e., undertake multiple tasks simultaneously) and/or switch quickly from task to task so the number of actual hours per day they spend using these technologies may be reduced. (p. 8)

Students will poll their peers to find an answer to the overarching question, "How much time do students in our school spend using technology when they are not in school?" Students will make a questionnaire to survey their campus, divide questions among groups, create a time line for gathering data, and determine how many responses they will need to gather to represent at least 35 percent of the student body. After data is collected, it will be analyzed using measures of central tendency (mean, median, mode, range). The lesson that follows will take place at this point of the unit study.

Students will then write and publish a two- to three-page report that includes an introduction, main points, a description of how the data was analyzed, and a conclusion. A printed copy of the report will be delivered to each member of the school board and school administrators as well as policymakers in the community such as legislators and civic leaders. In the case of the remake lesson, the report will be distributed via the Web.

Vocabulary Self-Collection Strategy (VSS) Lesson Plan

Materials

- Handout on measures of central tendency or pages focused on the topic in textbook
- Paper or poster board for word wall

Goal

Students will learn how measures of central tendency can be used to draw conclusions from data.

Rationale

Quantitative literacy is essential for members of a society as they make sense of mathematical information. These skills are used in daily life and can play a critical role in important life choices such as making purchases, securing job-related benefits, voting for political candidates, or engaging in sports or other recreational events.

Curriculum Standard (from National Council of Teachers of Mathematics)

- Student understands patterns, relations, and functions, and selects and uses appropriate statistical methods to analyze data. To do this, the student represents, analyzes, and generalizes a variety of patterns with tables, graphs, words, and when possible symbolic rules; the student finds, uses, and interprets measures of center and spread, including mean and inter-quartile range.

Objectives

- Students will identify and record unfamiliar math terms that are necessary to know and use when analyzing and summarizing data sets.
- Students will define unfamiliar math terms through class discussion of concepts, applications, and examples.

Vocabulary Self-Collection Strategy (VSS) Lesson Plan (cont'd)

Activities

- Introduction: Show students a graph of a normal distribution and ask what they think it means. Accept all ideas but do not explain what a normal distribution is.
- Activity 1: Give students handout describing measures of central tendency. (This could be a section of their textbook or a teacher-created handout.)
- Activity 2: Ask students to silently read and to write down any terms that are new or unfamiliar to them as they read. Inform them that they will keep a running list of these terms as they work on the project.
- Activity 3: Ask students to call out words from their list, and as they do, write those on the board, a transparency on an overhead projector, or on a computer screen that is connected to a digital projector. (Before the next day, write or print these words in very large font size and post them on a wall to create a word wall.) Add any words or phrases that you think should be on the list.
- Closure: Show the normal distribution graph again. This time, explain central tendency using a simple example like the range of shoe sizes in the room. Choose one or two of the words to define and ask students to write notes by the words on their list.

Modification

The VSS is designed to help all learners build vocabulary. Advanced students may have fewer words on their list while struggling learners may have more. Using a word wall provides the needed reinforcement for struggling learners. English language learners (ELLs), in particular, will have multiple opportunities to practice categorizing—or sorting—words into families such as *people*, *places*, and *ideas*. Word sorts can be closed (the teacher provides the categories) or open (students examine a list of words and create their own categories). The teacher can also encourage ELLs and struggling learners to draw symbols and figures in their notes to augment the meaning of the words they collected.

Assessment

Complete formative evaluations through discussions with students, questioning and listening for proper use of terms as students talk and work with each other.

How Is a Good Purposeful Writing Lesson Plan Made Better?

We see the purposeful writing frame as characterized by the digital native's aim to refine, order, revise, and edit what he is intending to communicate. When what is communicated is captured on paper, refining and revising typically entails peer editing, and the teacher may take the role of the evaluator of a finished product. The report produced by Scott's class as a result of this lesson, fortunately, will inform a community that extends beyond the classroom. The refining, ordering, revising, and editing that occurs, even in the most traditional sense, is not simply an exercise for a teacher-assigned grade. When this kind of purposeful writing happens in a digital sense, that is, in a technology-supported context, the roles of peers and of the teacher, in particular, take on a different dimension. Rather than being an evaluator, the teacher is more like a stage director, making sure that key lines are learned and rehearsed, props are in the right places, and everyone does his or her part. Like a performance, the final product is intended for public view.

By using VSS to select and list terms that are new to him, Scott will begin to enter the concept of central tendency into his long-term memory, somewhat like lines in a play are internalized. And by applying these terms in a report-writing activity that mimics what is done by professional polling groups, the newly acquired information will become procedural knowledge. That is, he will learn the tools and skills of professionals, and like them, he will use those for an authentic purpose: to inform his community of his findings. Among professionals who rely heavily on numeracy—researchers, engineers, architects, astronomers, accountants, mathematicians— writing technical reports is how findings, conclusions, and

theories are explained and disseminated. When these professionals' findings are delivered with technology, that information becomes multimodal. NASA's website, www.nasa.gov, and www.webmd.com, a site for medical information, illustrate how technical information is presented in the professional world through use of text, sound, video, or a combination of these formats. Scott and his peers know this kind of delivery of technical information best since they are quite at home on the Web. They may not be quite as aware of the work behind the product, though. Showing digital natives how the technical knowledge they are reading and viewing online began with knowing the terms and concepts that are used for a specific purpose and with a specific audience in mind and how information (words, images, graphs, etc.) was sculpted for a Web audience can make writing in math class more meaningful. Writing in this manner is purposeful writing.

Using Digital Forms of Data Gathering and Statistical Analysis

Identifying and listing unfamiliar terms through the VSS strategy and reinforcing that with a word wall will greatly help to clarify abstract and seemingly analogous terms like *mean*, *median*, and *mode*. Scott, who likely travels effortlessly through online environments, would be doubly motivated by building a **cyber word wall**, an online version of a word wall. He could add another dimension to the cyber word wall by creating and attaching a video (see www.animoto.com or www.jingproject.com) that explains terms such as *mean*, *median*, *mode*, *range*, *outlier*, and others.

Cyber Word Wall

A cyber word wall is like a physical word wall in the classroom, but it is online. It is a collection of terms and their meanings that can be created in a wiki or blog and that can be accessed by the creator, by people given access to it by the creator, or by anyone on the Web.

He could post his video on YouTube or TeacherTube to add to the collection of how-to videos, or tutorials, that are available there for students as they search for more information about math concepts and procedures. Data-gathering tools such as Survey Monkey (www.surveymonkey.com) could help him quickly create a survey and email it to others to complete online. Scott, like others his age, is comfortable with social networking systems and may enjoy inputting the data he gathers into an online collaborative spreadsheet like that available through Google docs or www.numsum.com. The spreadsheet would be accessible to students in his class, his town, his state, the nation, or other nations—students who may be gathering the data along with him. He might even conduct a survey to gather data from teen avatars, the cartoonlike people who live in a virtual online world and who are created by teens. (See http://teen.secondlife.com.) Such online methods and gamelike structures are much more engaging to today's digital natives than traditional forms of learning. As Marc Prensky (2001) reminds us,

> Digital Natives accustomed to the twitch-speed, multitasking, random-access, graphics-first, active, connected, fun, fantasy, quick-payoff world of their video games, MTV, and Internet are *bored* by most of today's education, well meaning as it may be. But worse, the many skills that new technologies *have* actually enhanced (e.g., parallel processing, graphics awareness, and random access)—which have profound implications for their learning—are almost totally ignored by educators. (p. 5)

What Is a Good Digital Version of a Purposeful Writing Lesson?

Imagine what the Rocket Boys would have created had they had today's computers to use in 1957. How would purposeful writing (and the VSS strategy) have looked had they used movies, graphics, or interactive links?

VSS Lesson Plan—The ReMake

Materials

- online access to a wiki, blog, or school Web page
- *Pisay* movie trailer—www.youtube.com/watch?v=zuXGrlWDZ5I

Goal

Students will learn how measures of central tendency can be used to draw conclusions from data.

Rationale

Quantitative literacy is essential for members of a society as they make sense of mathematical information. These skills are used in daily life and can play a critical role in important life choices such as making purchases, securing job-related benefits, voting for political candidates, or engaging in sports or other recreational events.

Curriculum Standard (from National Council of Teachers of Mathematics)

- Student understands patterns, relations, and functions, and selects and uses appropriate statistical methods to analyze data. To do this, the student represents, analyzes, and generalizes a variety of patterns with tables, graphs, words, and when possible symbolic rules; the student finds, uses, and interprets measures of center and spread, including mean and inter-quartile range.

Objectives

- Students will identify and record unfamiliar math terms that are necessary to know and use when analyzing and summarizing data sets.
- Students will define unfamiliar math terms through class discussion of concepts, applications, and examples.

VSS Lesson Plan—The ReMake (cont'd)

Activities

- Introduction: Show students movie trailer from the movie *Pisay* (2005; see trailer at www.youtube.com/watch?v=zuXGrlWDZ5I), a film about eight Philippino high school science students growing up in the turbulent time when the Marcos dictatorship was ousted by the 1986 People Power Revolution and Cory Aquino's new government assumed power. Then post this excerpt from the movie: "Those on the right side of the normal curve are the winners. Inside each side of the normal curve, there are smaller normal curves. No matter which side you're on in that smaller normal curve inside the right side of the major normal curve, you're still a winner!" Ask students to comment on what is meant by a "normal curve" and what the excerpt might mean.

- Activity 1: Ask students to go online and explore "measures of central tendency" (to engage in inside writing).

- Activity 2: Ask students to read and gather information and to post any terms that are new or unfamiliar to them on the class wiki under the heading "Cyber Word Wall." Inform students that they will keep a running list of these terms as they work on the project. Add any words or phrases that you think should be on the list.

- Activity 3: Explain central tendency and choose one or two of the words to define. Invite students to take personal notes in preparation to work with their peers as they post/revise/edit definitions on the cyber word wall. (Repeat this step the next day, and explain concepts with simple examples, such as the range of shoe sizes in the room.)

- Closure: Show *Mean, Median, Mode, and Range* movie in www.brainpop .com. Ask students to continue to refine cyber word wall by adding images, videos, links to other sites, etc.

VSS Lesson Plan—The ReMake (cont'd)

Modification

As in the original lesson, the remake offers opportunities for all students to build vocabulary. The cyber word wall can be modified to include supports like teacher-added hints about words or a list of websites to visit for each word that is posted. Spanish-speaking ELLs, in particular, can reinforce newly learned vocabulary by watching animated movies in www.brainpop.com's Spanish version.

Assessment

Complete formative evaluations by periodically checking the content of the cyber word wall and through discussions with students, questioning and listening for proper use of terms as students talk and work with each other.

In this lesson remake, writing in online spaces to communicate information means using the appropriate vocabulary, graphics, and other visuals for an intended audience. Add to this purposeful writing frame the collaborative spirit of making sense with others who are also online—an extension of the responsive writing frame described in Chapter 3. Collaboration and writing purposefully can and should extend outside the classroom world. Digital natives like Scott are accustomed to seeking like-minded people on the Internet to ask questions and offer answers, and ultimately to collaboratively construct knowledge together. Engaging in such online discourse communities, of course, means Scott and his peers need to have command of the language of that community. For instance, they could go to www.Math2.org's message board, a place for avid mathematicians to engage in ongoing exploration of the multiple ways math problems can be solved. Knowing the vocabulary of this discourse community is certainly important, so Scott's cyber word wall may become a helpful reference as he interacts with online mathematicians. He can also use available Web 2.0 tools to add graphs and graphics to his message in order to make his thinking crystal clear and, consequently, more powerful. An example is the online summary he and his peers created for this lesson. That data can be supplemented with bar graphs, histograms, and circle graphs that can easily be created using online tools like Numsum (www.numsum.com) and Google Docs spreadsheets (http://docs.google.com), or software like InspireData. In the case of Numsum and Google Docs spreadsheets, he can work collaboratively with others in real time or asynchronously. They can add to, discuss (using a chat room–like tool), and share their spreadsheets with selected people or the Web-using world. Just as they engaged in a communal cyber word wall, they can engage in a communal building of information, something they already do outside of school.

Ideally, they would take their new knowledge of how to create a cyber word wall to their out-of-classroom life. Digital natives have learned to create languages for topics like gaming and texting and will continue to name their world as they grow older. Creating their own cyber word wall for words they use will help them grow into their online discourse communities. Precision and logic in language is critical in conversations that occur in a lobby in a multiplayer game, for instance, where players from across the world meet with each other and must accurately use terms to make sense to each other. This is a large and growing 21st century discourse community. To become a member of it, a gamer needs to know the gaming language. Likewise, to become a successful member of a classroom community, a student needs to know the academic language.

While Scott and his peers are for the most part exploring general math concepts and procedures in this remake lesson to satisfy requirements of a math class, they are communicating with the kind of language that those who use math in their professions use. They are doing it in a setting they find intriguing and real, and more important, they are using the tools that professionals are using to be efficient (online surveys), to be accurate and clear (graphics and animation), and to disseminate information (Web 2.0).

How Do We Know
That Scott Is Learning?

Chapters 2 and 3 focus on student groups at two Title I–eligible schools in a large rural school district. The district has implemented a relatively conservative technology-use policy for its students and teachers. Students make frequent trips to computer labs for classroom activities and have access to library computers before school, during lunch, and after school. They are allowed Internet access, so each student is given a log-in student ID and school-assigned password. Their computer use, especially when online, is monitored closely by teachers, teacher assistants, librarians, and the campus technology coordinator.

For the third study, we decided to visit a middle school in an urban school district that offers the technology challenges many teachers experience—limited access to computers, little or no support from other staff members, and frequent computer maintenance and repair issues. The district we selected has a much more restrictive technology-use policy than the district referenced earlier. Most notable is the rule that students are not allowed to access the Internet on their own. Teachers must make prior arrangements for students to visit online environments, and access is usually restricted to publishing company–sponsored websites that provide additional practice for lessons found within the traditional textbooks.

These limitations definitely create obstacles for our proposed technology-enriched lessons, but we are certain that teachers (with help from their students) can find ways to work within restrictive environments. It is a natural instinct for 21st century students to seek out technology and to connect with their peers, and it is to our advantage to learn the adaptive habits of the digital natives.

To test the math lesson makeover, we asked three eighth-grade students—Stephen, Brendon, and Laila—to create the cyber word wall we envisioned. Stephen and Brendon consider themselves excellent math students. According to Stephen, "All I have to do is listen to the teacher. When I hear math, it makes sense to me." Laila, on the other hand, considers herself an average student who must frequently ask the teacher and other students to reexplain math concepts and assist her when solving problems.

To begin the makeover lesson, we began with an open conversation about learning and understanding vocabulary words in a math class. All three eighth graders agreed that learning new words for math is important, but they also pointed out that learning new vocabulary for math is not the same as learning new vocabulary in language arts, science, or social studies classes. Learning math vocabulary means learning procedures. Laila explained by saying, "A teacher will tell you a word, like *sum*, and then she'll tell you that when you see that word, it means you're supposed to add." Stephen agreed. "In math, part of understanding the definition of a word is understanding what you're supposed to do. If you see *difference*, you're supposed to subtract."

When these students were asked to consider the possibility of working with digital tools to explain the meanings and applications of math vocabulary words, Laila instantly responded with, "Well, first we could create a class website, and then we could create a math section where we can list and explain words that we're learning in math." Stephen and Brendon liked the idea, but then the reality of their school's technology policy hit. They encountered a major obstacle—no Internet access—but they quickly began the work of finding a way around their technological limitations.

Stephen, Brendon, and Laila still liked the idea of creating a website. The major questions became how to gain access and how to create a digital writing space for themselves and their classmates. Undaunted, they asked their teacher (who is required to maintain a Web page within the school's website) if she would allow them to add a class notes section on her page. The teacher agreed, but she wisely pointed out that they must reach an understanding of how the students would add and edit content on *her* page. The students and teacher negotiated terms and agreed that all work on the page must be done within the classroom. She would log in and supervise each student while he or she contributed to or edited the class's cyber word wall. Just like other visitors to the school's website, students would be able to view their teacher's page and their word wall from remote locations such as the library and home.

The students and teacher were satisfied with the agreement they reached. The students would be allowed to work within the online environment, and the teacher would be able to maintain control as her students added a valuable classroom resource to her Web page. For the students, the primary goal of the negotiations was not simply to gain online access but to be given the opportunity to work collaboratively in developing a tool that would reflect the collective knowledge of the class.

To begin the project, the teacher developed a system in which she introduced new vocabulary words and then asked specific students to work together to develop definitions and examples of the new words for the cyber word wall.

We watched as Stephen, Brendon, and Laila tackled *mean, median,* and *mode.* Stephen added the first entry by writing basic definitions. He wrote,

> When you're working with an arrangement of numbers, you can find the mean, median, and mode of the numbers. The mean is the average of the numbers. The median is the middle number. The mode is the number that is used most.

For Stephen, the text-based definitions were enough. "I've practiced these for a long time, so I know what they mean, and I know what I'm supposed to do." For Laila and Brendon, however, Stephen's definitions alone were not sufficient. The three students began a conversation, and Stephen could tell that he had not clearly defined the words for his classmates. He had not achieved the purpose of the cyber word wall—to communicate information clearly. This was an important realization for Stephen. He wanted to make sure that his classmates understood what he was saying, so he began to listen to their conversations and to ask questions until he knew what could be added to the word wall to further define the words. To help Brendon and Laila better understand *mean, median,* and *mode,* Stephen added examples of how to work with numbers to identify each term. And then he turned to Laila and Brendon for another conversation.

By this point, Brendon and Laila remembered that they had worked with these concepts before. Stephen's connections of words to examples were all his partners needed to reactivate prior knowledge. According to Brendon, "Yeah, I learned how to do that a long time ago. Everybody learns how to average their grades."

Stephen had accomplished his goal and had achieved the purpose of the cyber word wall. "I can really tell when Brendon doesn't understand something. When we're working on a problem, he doesn't know what he's doing wrong. I keep watching and listening, and I keep explaining until he gets it right."

Stephen worked primarily to clarify meaning for his two group members, but his work benefited the whole class. His definitions and examples can now be accessed from home computers. His original content on the Web page also became the foundation for future revisions from other classmates as the definitions became more ingrained in their daily conversations.

The eighth graders we observed faced obstacles common in many 21st century schools. Fortunately, they were able to make the necessary adaptations to work in a digital world that reaches far beyond the boundaries of the traditional classroom. The greater accomplishment, however, is that the digital natives found a teacher who, like the Rocket Boys' Ms. Riley, recognizes the promise of a new age.

Chapter Summary

Stephen, Brendon, and Laila are proof that students have a genuine desire to be clearly heard and understood. It is important for students to understand that their opinions, ideas, and knowledge are best expressed and shared when they use the most precise language possible. As stated at the beginning of this chapter, it is not unusual for a student to want his peers and the adults around him ". . . to know exactly what I think."

Purposeful writing is how the intention of the writer becomes clear to the reader, and the writing captures that intention so well that a reader can grasp what the writer meant without confusion or trepidation. Using Web 2.0 tools like a wiki can help students internalize the labels for concepts and consequently be able to use them appropriately when they are sharing information with others. In the next frame, the purposeful writing goes beyond informing. The writer carefully selects how thoughts are arranged so that there is not only a clear purpose but also a desire to take action.

Purposeful Writing Practice in Social Studies, Science, and English Language Arts

To practice ways of remaking a lesson plan so that it addresses purposeful writing, use the sample math remade lesson as a guide to designing a plan that uses VSS in social studies, science, or English language arts.

Social Studies: In a social studies class, students can create a cyber word wall of the American Revolution. Throughout the study unit, ask students to create their own lists and categories and complete an open word sort. A cyber word wall that focuses on a pivotal time in history can be made even richer by adding images, maps, and links to other sites such as www. theamericanrevolution.org/. As an enrichment activity, ask students to create a mind map that shows connections between military leaders, battles, unsung heroes, major cities, political leaders, documents, ideas, and so on, and upload it into the class wiki.

Address this curriculum standard from the National Council for the Social Studies—Thematic Strand 2: Time, Continuity, and Change:

■ Social studies programs should include experiences that provide for the study of the ways human beings view themselves in and over time, so that the learner can:

● identify and describe selected historical periods and patterns of change within and across cultures, such as the rise of civilizations, the development of transportation systems, the growth and breakdown of colonial systems, and other.

Science: Ask students to create a cyber word wall that lists the numerous career opportunities for students who pursue advanced studies in science.

Introduce terms for scientists—*biologist*, *endocrinologist*, *physicist*, *neuroscientist*, and so forth—and ask students to define the terms and include images of prominent scientists (past and present) in each field. Ask students to continue construction of the cyber word wall by listing more examples of scientists and adding text, images, videos, and links throughout the year. As an added challenge, ask students to complete an open word sort with the terms they have collected. (This word study will also be an excellent opportunity for students to build upon and strengthen their knowledge of Latin and Greek roots.)

Address this content standard from the National Science Education Standards:

- As a result of activities in grades 5–8, all students should develop understanding of science as a human endeavor.

  - Women and men of various social and ethnic backgrounds—and with diverse interests, talents, qualities, and motivations—engage in the activities of science, engineering, and related fields such as the health profession.

English Language Arts: Ask students to create a cyber word wall of figurative language. Begin by providing a "starter list" of figurative language terms—*simile*, *metaphor*, *hyperbole*, and *personification*—and ask students to add to the list as new terms are encountered throughout the year. Students can also add examples of figurative language found as they read short stories, novels, poems, and essays by providing excerpts from the selections. Further challenge students by asking them to provide their own examples (text or image) of figurative language.

Address this curriculum standard from the National Council of Teachers of English:

- Students apply a wide range of strategies to comprehend, interpret, evaluate, and appreciate texts. They draw on their prior experience, their interactions with other readers and writers, their knowledge of word meaning and of other texts, their word identification strategies, and their understanding of textual features (e.g., sound-letter correspondence, sentence structure, context, graphics).

Table 4.1 Resources for Purposeful Writing

Purposeful Writing Thinking Processes	Web Links and Tools Used in Math ReMake Lesson

Refining	www.Math2.org
	    online discourse community
	
	www.animoto.com
	
	www.jingproject.com
	    sites for creating visuals for online conversations

Ordering	www.numsum.com
	
	http://docs.google.com
	    sites to organize and create visual
	    representations of data
	
	InspireData
	    software to organize and create visual
	    representations of data

Revising and Editing	www.wikispaces.com www.pbwiki.com online collaborative writing spaces

Discussion Questions

1. How can the remake lesson described in this chapter be modified to fit in your classroom and to meet the needs of your students? If you are not teaching yet, consider how the remake lesson could be modified for a classroom you have observed.

2. A cyber word wall can be a short-term project, or it can grow into a year-long project. Within the context of a classroom, when would it be appropriate to construct a cyber word wall that students may post to, edit, and revise for a limited period of time? When would it be appropriate to create a cyber word wall that students will continue to "build" throughout the entire school year?

3. What is an effective lesson that can be made better by using the VSS strategy and technology?

References

Applebee, A. N., & Langer, J. A. (2006). *The state of writing instruction in America's schools: What existing data tell us.* Retrieved March 29, 2009, from Center on English Learning & Achievement, University at Albany website: www.albany.edu/aire/news/State%20of%20Writing%20Instruction.pdf.

Fletcher, M. (2003). *Reading to learn concepts in mathematics: an action research project.* Mobile: University of South Alabama. (ERIC Reproduction Service No.ED482001).

Gordon, C., Franco, L. J., Sternberg, M., & Cramer, P. (Producers), Hickam, H. H., Jr., & Colick, L. (Writers), & Johnston, J. (Director). (1999). *October sky* [Motion picture]. USA: Universal Studios.

Hickam, H. (1998). *The rocket boys.* New York: Delacorte Press.

Information processing theory. (n.d.). Retrieved March 20, 2008, from http://en.wikipedia.org/wiki/Information_processing_theory.

Newmann, F. (1993). Crafting authentic instruction. *Educational Leadership, 50*(7), 8–12.

Piaget, Jean. (1926). *The language and thought of the child*. New York: Harcourt, Brace.

Prensky, M. (2001). Digital natives, digital immigrants. *On the Horizon, 9*(5), 1–6.

Principles and Standards for School Mathematics. (2000). Reston, VA: National Council of Teachers of Mathematics.

Rapp, M. (1986). The vocabulary self-collection strategy: Using student interest and world knowledge to enhance vocabulary growth. *Journal of Reading, 29*(7), 634–642.

Research Images, LLC, & Pew Internet and American Life Project. (2007). *Teens, technology and writing: Teen insights on writing and technology in their lives*. Old Lyme, CT: Author.

Solito, A. (Producer/Writer). (2005). *Pisay* [Motion picture]. Cinemalaya. Retrieved March 29, 2009, from www.youtube.com/watch?v=zuXGrIWDZ5I.

Steen, L. A. (2001). Mathematics and numeracy: Two literacies, one language. *Journal of the Singapore Association of Mathematics Educators, 6*(1), 10–16.

Social Action Writing

Key Elements in Chapter 5

Social Action Writing This frame of writing describes how students explore a topic of interest, collaborate to arrive at an understanding of it, take a stance toward it, and craft a multimedia production intended to move others to action. They combine forms of persuasion with digital tools to maximize their message.

Critical Theory In sociology, critical theory refers to an examination of how power is negotiated among groups of people and how social norms should be opposed if they cause or perpetuate oppression. Critical pedagogy encourages students to question the status quo and to take action in an effort to change viewpoints or practices that breed injustice.

Literature Circles This strategy is intended for group analysis of works of literature. Each member of the group has a particular role such as discussion leader, illustrator, or summarizer. Roles rotate as the group meets to discuss sections of the book the members are reading.

Digital Stories Digital stories are life stories told through the use of sound, photos, graphics, and music. The story is written and recorded. The voice recording is over-laid on photos, graphics, and/or movies. Movie Maker, iMovie, Photo Story 3, and similar software are excellent tools to use to create a digital story.

Writers inspire. They may be hiding behind their glasses, but they really care about the world.

Mackenzie, grade 6

Chapter Preview

The fourth frame of the writing experience—*social action writing*—focuses on what we consider the most powerful kind of communication. Social action writing is intended to bring awareness to a social issue and to persuade others to act. Students have convictions that are developed through a deep knowledge of the values a society holds and of how those values affect lives. Writing is how those convictions are most often expressed. Political speechwriters who write to persuade voters, advertisers who write to sell a product, clergy who write to inspire a congregation, and attorneys who write to persuade a jury use writing to develop ideas that appeal to reason as well as to feelings. Technology animates this kind of writing by enhancing messages with images, sounds, text, music, and voice. This chapter will explore how viewpoints are developed, opinions expressed, and actions carried out. We will describe the make-over of a tenth-grade English language arts lesson that uses literature to guide students in a social action writing frame.

What Is Social Action Writing?

Erin Gruwell, the teacher whose life story is depicted in the movie *Freedom Writers* (Swank et al., 2007), shows how young writers have changed the world. Erin, played by actress Hilary Swank, listens to Black, Latino, and Asian gang members who are steeped in hatred. These Long Beach teens live in a domestic war zone, their neighborhoods affected by rampant interracial gang violence. Ms. Gruwell gives these street soldiers a place to write their stories about their war and uses *Anne Frank: The Diary of a Young Girl* (Frank, 1993) to open their eyes to oppression, injustice, and hope. Like Anne Frank, students write diaries, which become the most powerful weapons the students possess. They use their writing to change their community and themselves by bringing public attention to the injustices that they see and gaining the attention of the media. Like the Long Beach teens whose stories about their lives brought awareness and change not only to their community but to the nation, teens in all schools can use writing to influence change. This kind of **social action writing** primarily means expressing a passion for fairness and justice, but it goes beyond that. It means using that expression to actively improve themselves, their homes, their neighborhoods, their communities, the nation, and the world.

Social Action Writing
This frame of writing describes how students explore a topic of interest, collaborate to arrive at an understanding of it, take a stance toward it, and craft a multimedia production intended to move others to action. They combine forms of persuasion with digital tools to maximize their message.

Today's adolescents have much to be passionate about in their post-9/11 lives: terrorism, global warming, gang violence, immigration, alternative energy, disease, animal rights, and more. They are also, of course, concerned about issues that are specifically related to being teens, like using social networking systems to develop friendships or relationships, or using cell phones and iPods at school. Helping teens examine how they feel about these issues is the first step toward showing teens how their writing can potentially change them and the lives of others.

How can teens actually change their world? More important, *why* should they change their world? Digital natives are quite unlike the generations before them. They are citizens living in a diverse world. "Multi" is the prefix of our time: multiliteracies, multicultural, multilingual, and multimodal. In the United States, minorities are rapidly becoming the majority, yet some of these cultural groups are still facing inequities in school and the workplace. Digital natives are growing up in an electronically connected world, and they are in many ways experiencing life in multiple dimensions. As a result, teens can work toward helping to promote equity, social justice, tolerance, and democracy. Unlike past generations of teens, digital natives receive news as it is happening—from cell phones rather than TV screens or radios. They view video created by other teens and adults around the world. They communicate easily and inexpensively with people they may never meet who are living in places they may never visit. They engage in real-time events like tweeting, plurking, and live video streaming while sitting in front of computers. The results of the 2006 NetDay survey of almost 233,000 students (see www.tomorrow.org) show that more than half of our middle schoolers communicate electronically with students from other schools, states, and countries. That more than half of our adolescents are doing this means that a myriad of worldviews are being exchanged online. Because they have easy access to a cyberculture and because they can create messages in multimedia, digital natives, unlike any group before them, are uniquely empowered and equipped to be agents of change.

Had philosopher Paulo Freire known about Ms. Gruwell and the Freedom Writers, he might have sent her an email message praising her work. Freire (1998) once wrote, "One of the tasks of the progressive educator, through a serious, correct political analysis is to unveil opportunities for hope, no matter what the obstacles may be. After all, without hope there is little we can do" (p. 3). Many contemporary literary scholars, people who advocate theory-based methods of studying literature in our schools, would no doubt also applaud the social action writing Ms. Gruwell's students did, nodding in approval of the use of *Anne Frank: The Diary of a Young Girl* as a lens from which to view their own lives.

As in the frames that led to this one—inside writing, responsive writing, and purposeful writing—digital native writers engaging in social action writing read, respond to, and take a meaningful role in the unfolding of their real and virtual environments. Literature provides an arena for these writers to envision roles, to "read" from different perspectives, and to engage in writing that is intended to initiate action toward righting an injustice. A popular strategy for exploring literary works, and one that could be used to explore literary technique as well as intention, is literature circles (Daniels, 1994). It will be addressed in a tenth-grade lesson using three well-known classic and contemporary novels: *The Giver* (Lowry, 1993), *Brave New World* (Huxley, 1932), and *Fahrenheit 451* (Bradbury, 1953).

How Does Critical Theory Fit in Social Action Writing?

Writing for a purpose, the third frame of the writing experience, focuses on how purposeful writers compose representations of their understanding using a defined format. Writers craft conclusions drawn after carefully sifting through information. They edit each other's writing to make sure that they use precise language to logically explain what they know to a particular audience. Similarly, social action writing is about audience, only this time, the writer's purpose goes beyond informing the reader. This frame of writing is about becoming a change agent. In order to do that, a writer must bring clarity to the power struggles that exist in societies by recognizing how forces sometimes silence particular groups within a society. Founders of the Centre for Social Action, an international organization, have for more than two decades advocated for educating students to be change agents. In *Writing for a Change* (National Writing Project, 2006), the Centre for Social Action and the National Writing Project define "Social Action" methods in this way:

> Social Action is a process whereby young people consider *what* issues and problems concern them, analyze *why* they exist, consider how they can act to change them, take these actions, and then reflect on what they have done and what has changed. (p. 5)

The Centre's underlying belief is that "all people have the right to be heard, to define the issues that are facing them, and to take action on their own behalf; and the expectation that all people have skills, knowledge, and experience they can use to address problems they face" (p. 5). This perspective aligns well with those held by scholars who write about **critical theory**. Critical theory in education is generally explained as a way of seeing the world from different perspectives in order to examine how text empowers or disempowers particular groups of people and how social norms are created and preserved in writing. Critical theory emerges from a number of traditions such as sociology, literacy, and anthropology. Douglas Kellner (2006) proposes a critical theory of education that draws from all critical philosophical traditions. He suggests that students who are growing up in an electronically connected world are also living in a global economy, a fragile environment, and post-9/11 insecurity. He notes that young people,

Critical Theory

In sociology, critical theory refers to an examination of how power is negotiated among groups of people and how social norms should be opposed if they cause or perpetuate oppression. Critical pedagogy encourages students to question the status quo and to take action in an effort to change viewpoints or practices that breed injustice.

like the Freedom Writers, can make a difference. Teachers can assist these young global citizens by showing them how to view the world through different lenses and by bringing the knowledge of philosophers and theorists who have themselves changed the world through writing.

Teachers who are comfortable with critical theory envision the classroom not as a place where information is delivered to students but as a gathering where knowledge means making sense of the world and actively engaging in ways to make it just, harmonious, and fruitful. Critical pedagogy, then, is this kind of practice—a learning environment that creates spaces for teachers and students to use available tools to examine the world through multiple lenses, to examine themselves and see how similar or different they are from the rest of humanity. In the high school English classroom, for instance, *literary* theory, a way of looking at literature from a critical theory perspective, establishes occasions for students to critically analyze literature from different worldviews. In her book *Critical Encounters in High School English*, Deborah Appleman (2000) proposes that all high school students use literary theory to make sense of literature. She discusses how she asks students to look through driving sunglasses and describe what they see. Students note the difference in color—reds stand out, greens are greener. She asks them if the glasses changed the true colors and then hands out summaries of literary theory and explains that "what the sunglasses did for green and red, literary theory does for the texts we read. It provides lenses designed to bring out what is already there but what we often miss with unaided vision" (p. xvi). Like the sunglasses, the theories do not create what is not there. They help to make what is there clear.

When students examine how text has power, and how writers' perspectives are skillfully and deliberately delivered in writing, they are engaging in an ancient method of analyzing messages and how they persuade others to act. The Greek philosopher Aristotle is considered the father of rhetoric, the art of persuasion and argumentation. In very simple terms, he said that an *argument*, or a persuasive statement, is built on ethos, pathos, or logos. *Ethos* means appealing to reverence. *Pathos* means appealing to emotion. *Logos* means appealing to reason. Young people use these tools all the time.

For instance, a teen who wants a laptop for Christmas might try to convince parents to buy one by noting that it is necessary for students who are college bound and that all honors students have one (ethos). He may explain that he is the only one of his friends who doesn't have one and is often teased about being "left behind" (pathos). Or he may find data online to show what percentage of high school students own laptops, how many college students have them, and how prices have come down in the last two years (logos). A skillful writer would compose an argument for a laptop using all three tools. A more skillful writer will consider which approach will be most effective given the nature of the audience. A skillful digital native will add sound, images, video, and music to add dimension to the argument. It is the role of the teacher to channel what teens already know about argumentation to social action writing and guide them to a deep understanding of the complexity of their world and a genuine concern for making it better for all.

Imagine Emma, a tenth grader who is learning about the power struggles that are captured in history books, daily news reports, and literature. Her *self*-image is beginning to unfold as she compares her notions of the world with that of others. One way to do that is to engage her in a study of contemporary and classical novels that critically examine ageless issues such as finding identity, questioning norms, and taking risks. Giving her opportunities to examine these issues through different lenses will open a window into her own convictions and give her the tools to help her shape her world through writing.

What Is a Good Social Action Writing Lesson?

To teach students the three modes of persuasion—ethos, pathos, and logos—Emma's teacher assigns a collection of three novels. The novels— *The Giver* (Lowry, 1993), *Brave New World* (Huxley, 1932), and *Fahrenheit*

451 (Bradbury, 1953)—are well-known for their provocative, often controversial themes—themes that are similar despite the time periods in which the novels were written.

To begin the study unit, students are invited to select a novel and form **literature circles** with students who have chosen the same novel. (To learn more about literature circles, visit www.literaturecircles.com/ article1.htm.) To focus their

Literature Circles
This strategy is intended for group analysis of works of literature. Each member of the group has a particular role such as discussion leader, illustrator, or summarizer. Roles rotate as the group meets to discuss sections of the book the members are reading.

reading, each group is assigned a critical lens through which to read and discuss the novel. Groups are assigned a feminist, Marxist, or reader response lens and each group receives a one-page description of the theory. Emma's group, for example, reads *Fahrenheit 451* after reading the handout on feminist theory. While they read, each student engages in inside writing, and the internal discussions move out and into the group. The group's discussions allow each member to test perceptions and shape opinions. Their reflections are recorded in reader's journals. To complete the novel study, Emma's teacher asks each group to create a publication that contains two messages—(1) a concern or hope for the future, and (2) a call for change.

The sample lesson that follows is designed for one to three days and would be part of a larger unit plan. Prior to doing this lesson, students would have met in their literature circles and discussed the three theoretical perspectives—feminist theory, Marxist theory, and reader response theory—and how the literature they read can be viewed from these perspectives. They would have shared reflections, insights, and concerns discovered through their critical analyses. This discussion would have led to the group's identification of a societal issue that is present in the selected novel and that may be present in modern society. They would then have researched teacher and student-selected magazine articles, brochures, and newspaper clippings (and possibly websites, blogs, and wikis) to uncover underlying messages. Students would then list elements of persuasion (ethos, pathos, logos) they believe were used. This list would be used to create rubrics for examining and/or evaluating the students' writing. In the case of the original version of the plan, the following lesson would focus on creation and dissemination of a brochure, which may be created using a word processing program. In the make-over, students create a digital story. Pink (2006) stresses that telling stories is essential in what he calls the Conceptual Age. He explains that what matters in our fact-rich times is "the ability to place these facts in context and to deliver them with *emotional impact*" (p. 103). Digital stories are the vehicle for that. Through **digital stories**, writers can present facts within stories that can deliver powerful messages—messages that can move audiences to act.

Digital Stories

Digital stories are life stories told through the use of sound, photos, graphics, and music. The story is written and recorded. The voice recording is overlaid on photos, graphics, and/or movies. Movie Maker, iMovie, Photo Story 3, and similar software are excellent tools to use to create a digital story.

Literature Circles Lesson Plan

Materials

- class sets of three novels

- handouts on feminist theory, Marxist theory, and reader response theory (Students can create this with teacher guidance.)

- publications that exemplify each form of persuasion to facilitate discussion and analysis and to serve as models

Goal

Using forms of persuasion, students write to increase awareness of a societal issue, to advocate for change, and to persuade others to take an active role.

Rationale

Students should recognize and develop their potential to create change within their classrooms, their communities, and their world. Knowing how authors do that through their novels will help students see the power of their own writing.

Curriculum Standard (from National Council of Teachers of English)

- Students use spoken, written, and visual language to accomplish their own purposes (e.g., for learning, enjoyment, persuasion, and the exchange of information).

Objective

Students will design and write a publication to heighten awareness of a societal issue and to advocate for change.

Literature Circles Lesson Plan (cont'd)

Activities

- Introduction: Read a news clipping about the death of Alexander Solzhenitsyn, the Russian Nobel Prize–winning author who wrote the following in *The First Circle* (1997), his novel about inmates in one of Stalin's "special camps" for scientists who were deemed politically unreliable but whose skills were essential: "A great writer is, so to speak, a secret government in his country." Lead a short discussion about this quote.

- Activity 1: Ask literature circle groups to identify an audience and list points to support an argument for or against a position regarding a societal issue they selected to examine.

- Activity 2: Each member of the circle will be responsible for one of the three modes of persuasion and will lead a discussion. Ask groups to determine the most appropriate form of persuasion for their argument—ethos, pathos, or logos.

- Activity 3: Ask groups to collaboratively compose a draft that presents the argument, is intended to heighten awareness, and advocates for change.

- Closure: Ask groups to read portions of their drafts aloud and explain their reasoning. Tell them they will have more time to edit and revise the draft and create a brochure that will be distributed to the school/community.

Modifications

A number of student-centered practices that address diversity are the foundation of this lesson: project-centered learning, collaboration, connecting with text, and structure. Most important, individual voices are melding to create a consensus and a unified call for action. Their life stories are fueling a thoughtfully and purposefully constructed argument. As is the case with all the lessons presented, resources in multiple languages should be made available. In addition, the novels could be selected according to student interest and reading ability.

Assessment

Formative assessment: teacher observations and questioning, class-negotiated rubrics for evaluation of writing

How Is a Good Social Action Writing Lesson Made Better?

During this lesson, students learn how to interpret text and to find meaning by reading through a critical lens. They are encouraged to express their opinions, to challenge and empower other members of the group, to recognize a need for social change, and finally, to become knowledgeable and purposeful advocates for change. As it is, this lesson can create the kind of student-guided learning environment that critical theorists might envision. While the literature circles are at work and, more important, when students are writing, the teacher becomes a silent partner. In the business world, the silent partner is a term used to describe a person who provides capital such as money, materials, supplies, time, location, and any other support needed for a team to design a plan to achieve a goal. In Emma's classroom, the teacher provides a different kind of capital—the knowledge of novels and rhetorical devices and a learning environment that encourages new perspectives and courageous voices. He takes a few steps back and positions himself behind his students, overlooking, encouraging, and supporting. He is mindful that his own values and beliefs should not become the driving force of each group. In *Writing for a Change* (National Writing Project, 2006), we are reminded that ". . . asking students what they think demands a willingness on the teacher's part to hear 'the kinds of truths that are most difficult to accept' rather than assuming that students share the teacher's concerns" (p. 84).

After the student-created papers or publications are collected, it is very likely that the work will end there. In an ideal situation, the materials produced would be disseminated within the school, a neighborhood, or a community to influence change or action. For some students, a change in dress code, a project to restore the local youth center, or an extension of weeknight curfews may be the goal. For many digital natives, however, there is a desire to accomplish more. They are connected to a global community, and a call for change can be heard in their towns as well as on the other side of the world.

When a teacher recognizes that a study of rhetorical devices has a far greater potential—that the lesson can grow into a global call for action and change—he must be ready to step into a digital classroom. He must be mindful that, through Web 2.0, the digital natives are empowered writers. They can bypass the school setting and the teacher's feedback, and they can post personal, powerful texts and multimedia presentations without the benefit of a teacher's expertise. It is definitely in the teacher's best interest to position himself as a partner who supports Emma as she creates and posts an argument. It is exciting to think of this "silent partnership" as a new way of doing business in classrooms of the 21st century.

Making a Difference in a Digital Way

Great authors awaken and inspire. As she reads *Fahrenheit 451*, for example, Emma might find herself deeply troubled by Mildred, the wife of the protagonist. Mildred hides her emptiness and insecurities by immersing herself in television images that offer hope and acceptance. Sound familiar? It probably is to Emma, who may begin to question the role of media in defining acceptance and happiness in today's society. With the realization that average teens fall short of the perfection touted in the media, an enlightened (and frustrated) Emma knows that she has the power to craft an argument that urges teens to recognize the fallacy of media-promoted perfection. In the digital world, Emma's message can combine the ancient art of persuasion with the modern tools of technology.

Luckily, Emma can find a multimedia program that fits her level of expertise. She might decide to create a presentation or tell a story on PowerPoint or use iMovie from Apple, or Microsoft's Photo Story 3 or Movie Maker 2. Depending on resources and accessibility, Emma could work with more complex movie editing programs such as Apple Final Cut or Adobe Premier. She could also use a relatively new online tool called Voice Thread.

Emma can become an advocate for change on a global scale. She can create a digital story that presents the ugly side of beauty and perfection, and as unsettling images move across the screen, Emma will remind her audience that *they* have the power to define what is beautiful within a society. With voice, images, and music she'll fashion a digital rhetorical argument. In his book, *Digital Storytelling: Capturing Lives, Creating Community* (2006), Joe Lambert, the founding director of the Center for Digital Storytelling, says, "By listening really well, we can open ourselves up to new perspectives, new solutions—not by one side winning the debate but by reframing our diverse connections to the big story in a way that creates consensus" (p. xxi).

What Is a Good Digital Version of a Social Action Writing Lesson?

The literature circles lesson remake has an identical goal and rationale as the original. The objectives, procedures, and materials, however, describe the creation of a digital story instead of a print publication. Because a digital story takes more time, the lesson remake may be longer than the original.

Literature Circles Lesson Plan—The ReMake

Materials

- class sets of three novels
- handouts on feminist theory, Marxist theory, and reader response theory (Students can create this with teacher guidance.)
- publications/websites (particularly, www.storycenter.org) that exemplify each form of persuasion to facilitate discussion and analysis and to serve as models
- photographs (collected from home or from online archives)
- scanner
- computers with Internet connection
- for future lessons, students may need digital voice recorders and/or video camcorders, multimedia production and/or editing program(s)

Goal

Using forms of persuasion, students write to increase awareness of a societal issue, to advocate for change, and to persuade others to take an active role.

Rationale

Students should recognize and develop their potential to create change within their classrooms, their communities, and their world. Knowing how authors do that through their novels will help students see the power of their own writing.

Curriculum Standard (from National Council of Teachers of English)

- Students use spoken, written, and visual language to accomplish their own purposes (e.g., for learning, enjoyment, persuasion, and the exchange of information).

Objectives

- Students will create a digital story that heightens awareness of a societal issue and advocates for change.
- Students will electronically distribute digital stories.

Literature Circles Lesson Plan—The ReMake (cont'd)

Activities

- Introduction: Tell students about the death of Alexander Solzhenitsyn, the Russian Nobel Prize–winning author who wrote the following in *The First Circle* (1997), his novel about inmates in one of Stalin's "special camps" for scientists who were deemed politically unreliable but whose skills were essential: "A great writer is, so to speak, a secret government in his country." Play a short audio sample (podcast) of his writing from www.notepods.com. Lead a short discussion about the quote and podcast.

- Activity 1: Ask literature circle groups to identify an audience and list points to support an argument for or against a position regarding a social issue they selected to examine.

- Activity 2: Each member of the circle will be responsible for one of the three modes of persuasion and will lead discussion. Ask students to examine examples of digital stories from the Center for Digital Storytelling (www.storycenter.org), select an audience, and construct an argument using the most appropriate form of persuasion—ethos, pathos, or logos.

- Activity 3: Ask students to draft their argument in a story format. The story should not exceed 400 words. Joe Lambert of the Center for Digital Storytelling suggests limiting a story/script to approximately 350 words. Digital stories are intended to be concise, so beginning with a set number of words is helpful. Ask students to gather and scan photographs or to locate and download Web images that are appropriate for the digital story.

- Closure: Ask groups to share their ideas for the digital story and read portions of what they have drafted. Tell them they will have more time to edit and revise the draft and create a digital story that will be uploaded on the school server, YouTube, TeacherTube, and/or other organization-based servers. (If unable to upload, students can burn copies of their digital stories onto DVDs and distribute them to intended audiences.)

Literature Circles Lesson Plan—The ReMake (cont'd)

Modifications

This remake clearly incorporates the student-centered practices that address diversity: project-centered learning, collaboration, connecting with text, and structure. It also allows for individual voices to create a consensus and a unified call for action as students weave life stories into a thoughtfully and purposefully constructed argument. The digital story can be written and recorded in a single language or a blend of languages, depending on the group's intention.

Assessment

Formative assessment: teacher observations and questioning class-negotiated rubrics for evaluation of digital story (See online resources for ideas for creating rubrics, particularly http://its.ksbe.edu/dst/#Rubrics and http://rubistar.4teachers.org/index.php.)

The social action writing experience described in the Literature Circles lesson extends the opportunity to learn about the power of words to an opportunity to learn about the power of words, sound, and visuals. That opportunity will also give Emma the tools to find her own convictions, to decide how to express them, and to feel empowered as she calls for change. Most important, the lenses from which she can now evaluate literature, or any form of artistic or technical expression, will inspire her to explore with a clear intention (inside writing), to insightfully contribute words, images, and sounds for group review (responsive writing), and to refine her message using just the right language for her audience (purposeful writing). To explore the track that Emma may chart as she finds her voice and a way to express it, imagine that Emma and her group decide to create a digital story about eating disorders like anorexia and bulimia. The group feels

Table 5.1 Suggested Steps for Creating a Digital Story

1. Import and arrange the collected images into the video editing program's time line and apply timings, effects, and transitions.

2. Select and download copyright-free music and import into the audio track of the program.

3. Read and adjust the script (the writing) to correspond with the images.

4. Record and import a voiceover into the second audio track.

5. Complete a final edit of the whole project. (This is a very intense process! Students will need to watch their stories over and over, tweaking timings, transitions, volume levels, etc.)

strongly that teen girls are victims of a profiteering fashion market. They may begin with a search online to find information about eating disorders and they can begin to collect information from sites like www .nationaleatingdiscorders.org and www.somethingfishy.org. The information includes text, photos, graphs, and video. They may then visit websites of popular fashion and find photos, graphics, and video that glamorizes bone-thin girls. Emma and her group will create a wiki space where they can begin to store their information and where they can begin to write their comments about what they are finding. The wiki will be a depository for the materials they will use as they create their digital story. Because it is on a wiki, they can access it, add to it, and edit it at anytime from anywhere. Once they have all that they need, they can sift through the collection and examine it through a feminist lens. As they determine the audience—peers, parents, educators, community leaders, business leaders—they will consider whether ethos, logos, or pathos or a combination is the best approach to take. And they will begin to write their four-hundred-word script. If they choose ethos, they may decide to interview and audiotape someone in the community who has a medical background and is knowledgeable about the topic, or they may choose to use information from sites like the two listed earlier. If they choose to take a logos approach, they may let the data speak for the cause—rising statistics, mortality rates, related diseases, and so forth. Sites like the ones sponsored by the National Institute of Mental Health (www.nimh.nih.gov) and the American Academy of Family Physicians (www.familydoctor.org) would be helpful. Most students would likely recognize the power of pathos for this particular project. Appealing to emotions is a natural choice. The personal story or stories of girls who have overcome an eating disorder can be quite moving, and there are numerous ones online. (See www.caringonline.com and www.healthdiaries.com.) Depending on the audience, one, two, or all forms of persuasion could guide the construction of the digital story. Emma and her group could assemble data, photos, personal stories, and graphics from their collection on the wiki as they collaboratively draft their story. In essence, they would create a storyboard together—text linked with visuals and the background music that will weave it all together. Once the four-hundred-word story is written, one or more group members will read it and record it. Using a program like Photo Story 3 (free online at www.microsoft.com), they would build a short multimedia production intended to persuade an audience to act against what the media has persuaded young women to do. Emma and her group now have the tools they need to write for social action and to broadcast their voices.

How Do We Know That Emma Is Learning?

Moving beyond the safe world of pen and paper or Word documents certainly requires a leap of faith, but the teacher who steps into the digital realm and allows his students to work with images, words, and music will not be disappointed. His students are masters at working with the tools of Web 2.0, and they have learned to use these tools effectively to convey their messages to a global audience. Digital natives have learned how to capture their "fifteen minutes of fame" by creating exceptionally sophisticated multimedia productions and posting them to YouTube, Facebook, and other social networking systems. True, a large number of adolescents create these short videos for purely egocentric purposes. They publicize pranks committed at fast-food restaurants and other public places. They record themselves singing their unique versions of rock classics. And after their videos are uploaded, they are happy with the knowledge that they have a presence in the digital universe. One simple click and their videos stream into homes on the other side of the world.

The digital natives who recognize the power of social action writing know that they can use their videos to raise public awareness of important issues. They know they can use images, music, and powerful words to express opinions, to challenge the status quo, and to advocate for change. Experienced teachers know that there are rewarding moments in their classrooms when students are emotionally charged and are eager to engage in an open dialogue to express their opinions and ideas. A provocative piece of literature can spark a heated debate about euthanasia, for instance. Data on the graduation rate from a local high school can create a heightened awareness of which students are most likely to succeed within the current education system. Immigration legislation can raise issues of fairness and civil liberties. When students are this invested in the learning, it is time for the teacher to challenge his students, to remind them that their voices and their words can be crafted into thoughtful arguments and that those arguments can bring about change, a very powerful message for an adolescent who often believes she has no voice.

In a particularly inspiring scene from *Freedom Writers* (Swank et al., 2007), Miep Geis, the Dutch citizen who hid Anne Frank and her family from the Nazis during World War II, travels from Germany to talk to the young writers. She reminds them that they, too, have the power to change the world. "We are all ordinary people, but even an ordinary secretary or a housewife or a teenager can within their own small ways turn on a small light in a dark room."

There will naturally be a concern that students who work with music and images to construct a message of change will lose sight of the objective. There is also the fear that the writing, the focus of the project, will become an afterthought as students work with multimedia programs. Our digital natives Lillian and Chris proved that writing *is* an integral part of the process, and it is the foundation from which all other artistic decisions are made.

Lillian, a loyal advocate of animal rights, is a soft-spoken teenager who likes to fade into the background of any classroom. It is remarkable to watch her transformation from quiet student to empowered defender. After she chose her topic, she looked for personal connections by sorting through a box filled with photos of family pets. Most of the photos are blurred, but Lillian looked at them fondly and instantly began to talk about where she lived and how old she was when she got the pet parakeet or the two dachshunds. The pictures became a chronological record of her life, and through our conversation, it was obvious that Lillian formed strong, emotional attachments with her pets. "We move a lot, and just when I finally get a good group of friends, we move again. My pets are the only part of my life that stays the same."

After Lillian sorted her photos, she scanned them and imported them into Photo Story 3. The images became her inspiration, and she began to write a script, simultaneously arranging words and images to match her message. When the first draft was complete, Lillian quietly read the script as she watched the images move across the monitor, and she continued to revise her words and images. She rearranged the images to create a progression of scenes that began with a full picture of her beloved dog, Augie, and ended with a close-up of his innocent face. Lillian became an editor of video and text. She deleted sentences from the script to keep her work compact and focused. She adjusted the timing of her presentation to give her audience a chance to make an emotional connection between the words and the images. "I kept reading the script to myself and watching the pictures because I knew what I wanted it to look like, and I knew what I wanted it to sound like. I just kept making changes until it all fit together."

It is important to point out that not all presentations have to change the world. Lillian, for example, shared her digital story with a local animal shelter, and they posted the story on their website. Lillian's story affected her immediate community, and that was enough for her.

Chris, a very outspoken, confident sophomore, instantly knew that his presentation would address environmental issues, specifically preserving our natural resources. Because he and his family often visit state and national parks, Chris has an abundance of personal knowledge and experience to bring to his project. He is also very experienced with a variety of multimedia applications, so he decided to work with an advanced movie-editing program to create a digital story. Like Lillian, Chris began by searching for personal photos from his family's travels, but he discovered that those photos had disappeared. They were lost during a divorce settlement, and after several failed attempts by his dad to send digital versions through email, Chris had to begin his project without images, a very interesting spot for a digital native. He was not concerned, however. "I just started writing. I know that when I write I see the pictures in my head, and I can go look for them on Google. It's OK if there are other people in them because I can take them out. I can make them my pictures."

And that is just what Chris did. He wrote a very powerful script about the natural beauty of our land. He found and edited images that enhanced his message. Chris combined his words and images with music and movement to create a digital story that has meaning at two levels. The first level is a very personal level for Chris. "I wanted to write a story about what it was like when my family was together, when we would go camping and swimming and things were good." The second level was created for a global audience, and Chris's message is clear. "We can't mess up what we have. We won't get a second chance."

It is not surprising that our digital natives, Lillian and Chris, used *pathos* to craft their arguments. Perhaps it is because adolescents instinctively know that if there's going to be change, you have to start with the heart.

Chapter Summary

In creating a digital story, students have a forum for expressing what they feel and a tool for changing how others feel. Brochures and other text-based products can be effective for this purpose, but digital natives are more comfortable using multimedia to persuade others by using ethos, pathos, and logos to frame multisensory arguments. Teachers who recognize this can create powerful lessons that can change how students operate in the classroom as well as how they engage in the unfolding of global events.

Novels like *Fahrenheit 451* and movies like *Freedom Writers* were created from the social action writing framework as are countless websites dedicated to promoting a cause. Books, movies, and websites can be used in the classroom to launch the cycle of the four frames of writing: inside writing (knowing self and connecting to world), responsive writing (exploring others' connections to world), purposeful writing (composing to make sense to others), and social action writing (being an advocate for change in their world). Each frame flows seamlessly into the next. And the circle—personal connection to advocacy—begins again.

Social Action Writing Practice in Social Studies, Science, and Math

To practice ways of remaking a lesson plan so that it addresses social action writing through digital stories, use the sample English remake lesson as a guide to designing a plan that incorporates literature circles or a similar grouping strategy in social studies, science, or math.

Social Studies: Ask student groups to create digital stories that speak to the nation's (or their community's) growing cultural diversity. Encourage students to consider themes such as acceptance and tolerance as they share ideas and develop stories. Challenge them to address important social and cultural issues such as immigration, education, economics, and globalization.

Consider the following curriculum standard from the National Council for the Social Studies—Thematic Strand IV: Individual Developement and Identity:

- Social studies programs should include experiences that provide for the study of individual development and identity so that the learner can:

    - articulate personal connections to time, place, and social/cultural systems.

    - identify, describe, and express appreciation for the influences of various historical and contemporary cultures on an individual's daily life.

Science: Ask student groups to create digital stories that address their observations, beliefs, and values regarding science and technology. Challenge students to recall personal and family health experiences and to address the implications of issues such as genetic engineering, stem cell research, bionics, or nanomedicine.

Consider the following content standard from the National Science Education Standards:

- Science and technology in local, national, and global challenges:

    - Science and technology are essential social enterprises, but alone they can only indicate what can happen, not what should happen. The latter involves human decisions about the use of knowledge.

    - Individuals and society must decide on proposals involving new research and the introduction of new technologies into society. Decisions involve assessment of alternatives, risks, costs, and benefits and consideration of who benefits and who suffers, who pays and gains, and what the risks are and who bears them. Students should understand the appropriateness and value of basic questions—"What can happen?"—"What are the odds?"—and "How do scientists and engineers know what will happen?"

Math: Ask students to gather data about government spending on defense, education, health, social programs, and so on, since 1950. Ask students to analyze the data to identify trends in federal spending and to make predictions about future spending. Using the results of the data analysis, ask students to discuss their perceptions of the federal government's spending, past, present, and future, and to consider the perceptions a government creates through its economic policies. Ask students to create digital stories that address their insights. Challenge students with questions such as, "Does federal spending accurately reflect your values and beliefs?" "If you could prioritize federal spending, what programs would you most strongly support?" and "How does federal spending affect you/your family?"

Consider the following standard from the National Council of Teachers of Mathematics:

- Formulate questions that can be addressed with data and collect, organize, and display relevant data to answer them.

- Select and use appropriate statistical methods to analyze data.

- Develop and evaluate inferences and predictions that are based on data.

- Understand and apply basic concepts of probability.

Table 5.2 Resources for Social Action Writing

Social Action Writing Processes	Web Links and Tools Used in English ReMake Lesson
Expressing	www.blogger.com www.wordpress.com online interactive journals
Challenging	www.wikispaces.com www.pbwiki.com online collaborative writing spaces
Advocating	Microsoft Photo Story 3 Microsoft Movie Maker Apple iMovie video editing programs

Discussion Questions

1. How can the remake lesson described in this chapter be modified to fit in your classroom and to meet the needs of your students? If you are not teaching yet, consider how the remake lesson can be modified to fit in a classroom you have observed.

2. It is important to remember that not all students will have a story they are willing to share. What accommodations can be made for students who do not feel comfortable sharing personal stories?

3. If you had the opportunity to create a digital story, what might be your topic? Why?

4. What is an effective lesson that can be made better by using literature circles/study circles and technology?

References

Appleman, D. (2000). *Critical encounters in high school English*. New York: Teachers College Press.

Bradbury, R. (1967). *Fahrenheit 451*. New York: Simon and Schuster.

Daniels, H. (1994). *Literature circles: Voice and choice in the student-centered classroom*. Portland, ME: Stenhouse.

Frank, A. (1993). *Anne Frank: The diary of a young girl* (B. Mooyaart, Trans.). New York: Bantam. (Original work published 1947)

Freire, P. (1998). *Pedagogy of hope*. New York: Continuum.

Huxley, A. (1946). *Brave new world*. New York: HarperPerennial.

Kellner, D. (1998). Multiple literacies and critical pedagogy in a multicultural society. *Educational Theory, 48*(1), 103–122.

Lambert, J. (2006). *Digital storytelling: Capturing lives, creating community* (2nd ed.). Berkeley, CA: Digital Diner Press.

Lowry, L. (1993). *The giver*. Boston: Houghton Mifflin.

National Writing Project. (2006). *Writing for a change*. San Francisco: Jossey-Bass.

Pink, D. (2006). *A whole new mind.* New York: Penguin Group.

Solzhenitsyn, A. (1997). *The first circle* (T. P. Whitney, Trans.). Evanston, IL: Northwestern University Press. (Original work published 1968)

Swank, H., Durning, T., & Morales, N. (Producers), & LaGravenese, R. (Writer/Director). (2007). *Freedom Writers* [Motion picture]. USA: Paramount Pictures, United International Pictures.

chapter 6

Ten of Tens

By thinking of learning in terms of the four frames of mind that attempt to explain the way digital natives write, any lesson can have a make-over. As in the popular TV and magazine make-overs of people and homes, knowledgeable designers and adequate resources are necessary. This chapter is a list of designers and resources, and it might be useful as a starting point for a plan to make adjustments to how writing is taught in our schools. We have collected ten lists, each containing ten people, resources, or ideas that could be considered when a lesson, a unit, or a curriculum undergoes a make-over. In the case of online resources, we selected websites that have had longevity or the promise of it.

Ten Quick Ways to Change One Part of a Lesson or Unit Plan

1. Use a YouTube or TeacherTube movie in the introduction to hook the learner.

2. Create a blog for you and your students to engage in dialogue.

3. Create a wiki for student groups to work on a collaborative project.

4. Show students how to use Son of Citation Machine (www.citationmachine .net) to create bibliographies for research papers and reports.

5. Set up a classroom in Nicenet (www.nicenet.org) or Moodle (www .moodle.org).

6. Include a podcast from www.notepods.com.

7. Ask students to use Photo Story 3 (free download) to create a digital story.

8. Use a social bookmarking site like del.icio.us (http://delicious.com/) to make selected websites available from any computer.

9. Find three copyright-free photo websites for students to use to find images for projects.

10. Do an online survey using a free online tool like www.surveymonkey.com.

Ten Examples of 21st Century Teaching

1. Middle and high school students across the United States use Web 2.0 tools to participate in global collaborative projects. See http://flatclassroomproject.wikispaces.com.

2. High school students in San Fernando, California, use multimedia tools to create powerful videos. See http://sfett.com/index.html.

3. High school students in Moanalua, Hawaii, integrate core curriculum with video and other media. See www.mohs.k12.hi.us/media-central/index2.html.

4. High school students in Napa, California, complete technology-based projects as they tackle complex, real-world problems. See www.newtechhigh.org/Website2007/index.html.

5. Science students in Washington and across the nation work with community members to collect biodiversity data and record in a national database. See http://depts.washington.edu/natmap.

6. Students in Aroostook County, Maine, interviewed local potato farmers and researched the potato industry and created a website to share their findings. See www.tateract.org.

7. Middle school students in Portland, Maine, investigated endangered species of their state and created a CD, *Fading Footprints*. See http://king.portlandschools.org/files/onexpedition/expeditionproducts/footprints/frameset/frame.htm.

8. High school students in Punxsutawney, Pennsylvania, maintain a wiki that serves as the hub for their science class activities. See http://mrsmaineswiki.wikispaces.com.

9. In Waco, Texas, eighth graders are integrating Whyville, a Web-based virtual world, into their career-exploration classes. See www.whyville.net/smmk/nice.

10. High school students in the Modesto, California, area are linked to students in Kyoto, Japan, in a cultural exchange via a virtual world environment. See http://pacificrimx.wordpress.com.

Ten Terms Every Teacher Should Know

1. Web 2.0
2. blog
3. wiki
4. podcast
5. instant messaging
6. texting
7. social network system
8. gaming
9. Creative Commons
10. Internet classroom assistant

Ten People to Google

1. David Warlick
2. Joe Lambert
3. Marc Prensky
4. Wesley Fryer
5. Alan November
6. Shawn Wheeler
7. Josie Fraser
8. Gail Hawisher
9. Cynthia Selfe
10. Margaret Roblyer

Ten Professional Organizations to Explore (and Join)

1. National Writing Project

2. International Society for Technology in Education

3. National Educational Computing Conference

4. National Council of Teachers of English

5. International Reading Association

6. National Council of Teachers of Mathematics

7. National Council of Teachers of Science

8. National Council of Social Studies Teachers

9. National Council of Teacher of Fine Arts

10. National Association for Bilingual Education

Ten Books to Read

1. Richardson, W. (2006). *Blogs, Wikis, Podcasts, and Other Powerful Web Tools for Classrooms.* Thousand Oaks, CA: Corwin Press.

2. Prensky, M. (2006). *Don't Bother Me, Mom, I'm Learning.* St. Paul, MN: Paragon House.

3. Cummins, J., Brown, K., & Sayers, D. (2007). *Literacy, Technology, and Diversity: Teaching for Success in Changing Times.* Boston: Pearson/Allyn and Bacon.

4. McCain, T., & Jukes, I. (2001). *Windows on the Future.* Thousand Oaks, CA: Corwin Press.

5. Lambert, J. (2002). *Digital Storytelling: Capturing Lives, Creating Community.* Berkeley, CA: Digital Diner Press.

6. Friedman, T. (2005). *The World Is Flat*. New York: Farrar, Straus and Giroux.

7. Warlick, D. (2004). *Redefining Literacy for the 21st Century*. Worthington, OH: Linwood.

8. Shamburg, C. (2007). *English Language Arts Units for Grades 9–12*. Washington, DC: ISTE.

9. Solomon, G., & Schrum, L. (2007). W*eb 2.0—New Tools, New Schools*. Washington, DC: ISTE.

10. Christensen, C. M., Johnson, C. W., & Horn, M. B. (2007). *Disrupting Class: How Disruptive Innovation Will Change the Way the World Learns*. New York: McGraw-Hill.

Ten Websites to Bookmark

1. Project Tomorrow: www.tomorrow.org

2. Wikipedia: www.wikipedia.com

3. PBS Teachers: www.pbs.org/teachers

4. Wisegeek: www.wisegeek.com

5. Commonsense Media: www.commonsensemedia.org

6. Story Chasers: http://storychasers.org

7. What Kids Can Do: www.whatkidscando.org

8. Classroom 2.0: www.classroom20.com

9. TeacherTube: www.teachertube.com/

10. Our Stories: http://ourstories.org

Ten Free Online Tools

1. Edublogs (blog): http://edublogs.org/

2. Wikispaces (wiki): www.wikispaces.com/

3. Animoto (video sharing): http://animoto.com/

4. Voice Thread (image, document, and video sharing): http://voicethread.com/

5. Blurb (book publishing): www.blurb.com/

6. Google Apps (combination of various collaborative tools): www.google.com/apps/

7. Num Sum (collaborative Web spreadsheets): http://numsum.com/

8. Ning (social networking): www.ning.com/

9. Moodle (course management system): http://moodle.org/

10. FreeMind (concept mapping): http://freemind.sourceforge.net/wiki/index.php/Main_Page

Ten Journals or Magazines to Review Frequently

1. *T.H.E. Journal*

2. *Learning and Leading with Technology*

3. *Edutopia*

4. *Educational Technology Magazine*

5. *Converge*

6. *eLearn Magazine*

7. *Technology and Learning Online*

8. *MultiMedia Schools*

9. *Ties*

10. *Tech Directions*

Ten Informal Classroom Investigations You Can Do

1. Take a survey of students to find out information about their use of technology.

2. Enhance one unit or lesson plan with a blog; download posts in the blog and look for increased use of subject-specific vocabulary to gauge how students' writing indicates the degree to which they are internalizing what they are learning.

3. Ask students to create a digital story related to a topic they are learning; interview a randomly selected small group in each class to find out what challenges they faced when they created their project and what they learned about their topics.

4. Keep a journal (on a blog or wiki, if you wish) and start with a statement of what you would like your students to do using technology; follow with a question about how you will achieve that. Write a response to the question and let that lead to daily or weekly reflections of your practice and ideas for activities.

5. Try three ideas described in the book. At the end of a unit, semester, or year, ask students which of the three activities they enjoyed most. Ask why. Draft a plan for the next time you teach the lesson(s).

6. Ask your students to interview a professional in the community (ages 22 to 42) to find out how they use technology to write at work—reports, messages, etc. Gather information collected and draw conclusions about real-world applications.

7. Record yourself giving a short lecture, post it on your blog, and ask students in one class to listen to it. Conclude the lecture with a question. Ask students to respond to the question by posting on the blog. Present the same short lecture live in another class. Ask students to respond to the question by writing on paper. Compare the length and quality of online and in-class responses.

8. Examine how one activity that you do regularly (journal writing, practice problem, vocabulary list, homework assignment, etc.) can be enhanced using a blog, wiki, or podcast. Compare student performance before the technology enhancement to student performance after enhancement.

9. Focus on one or two students who are low performing. Keep a reflective journal to document how they respond to learning activities after adding technology to a lesson. Note changes in grades and/or attitude.

10. Ask more tech-proficient students to form a committee to assist in Web 2.0 integration. After a lesson or activity, ask them to design a remake of the lesson or activity.

Index